# The Mentor & the Mentee

Patience Sakutukwa

Published by Bethel Publishing House, 2024.

While every precaution has been taken in the preparation of this book, the publisher assumes no responsibility for errors or omissions, or for damages resulting from the use of the information contained herein.

THE MENTOR & THE MENTEE

**First edition. September 8, 2024.**

Copyright © 2024 Patience Sakutukwa.

ISBN: 978-0796173232

Written by Patience Sakutukwa.

# Table of Contents

INTRODUCTION .................................................................... 1
Chapter 1 ............................................................................... 8
The Importance of Mentorship ............................................. 9
Chapter 2 ............................................................................. 12
Effects of Mentorship .......................................................... 13
Chapter 3 ............................................................................. 17
Signs That You Need a Mentor ........................................... 18
Chapter 4 ............................................................................. 21
Signs That You Are a Mentor .............................................. 22
Chapter 5 ............................................................................. 27
Identifying Your Mentor ..................................................... 28
Chapter 6 ............................................................................. 32
Identifying Your Mentee ..................................................... 33
PART II ............................................................................... 35
EXPLORING MENTORSHIP DYNAMICS ..................... 36
Chapter 7 ............................................................................. 37
Types of Mentors ................................................................. 38
Chapter 8 ............................................................................. 47
Types of Mentees ................................................................. 48
Chapter 9 ............................................................................. 51
Types of Mentorship ........................................................... 52
PART III .............................................................................. 55
SPECIALIZED MENTORSHIP ......................................... 56
Chapter 10 ........................................................................... 57
Traditional Mentorship ....................................................... 58
Chapter 11 ........................................................................... 61
Spiritual Mentorship ........................................................... 62
Chapter 12 ........................................................................... 67
Physical Mentorship ............................................................ 68
Chapter 13 ........................................................................... 70
Professional Mentorship ..................................................... 71

Chapter 14 ..................................................................................73
Creative Mentorship ..................................................................74
The Essence of Creative Mentorship ........................................76
The Impact ..................................................................................77
Chapter 15 ..................................................................................78
Marital Mentorship ...................................................................79
PART IV ......................................................................................82
MENTORSHIP IN VARIOUS CONTEXTS ........................83
Chapter 16 ..................................................................................84
Community Mentorship ..........................................................85
Chapter 17 ..................................................................................88
Global Mentorship ....................................................................89
Chapter 18 ..................................................................................93
Online Mentorship ....................................................................94
Chapter 19 ..................................................................................97
In-Person Mentorship ...............................................................98
Chapter 20 ............................................................................... 102
Academic Mentorship ............................................................ 103
Chapter 21 ............................................................................... 104
Cross-Cultural Mentorship ................................................... 105
PART V .................................................................................... 107
UNDERSTANDING MENTORSHIP IMPACT ............... 108
Chapter 22 ............................................................................... 109
Mentorship in the Era of Technology ................................. 110
Chapter 23 ............................................................................... 113
Navigating your Mentorship Journey .................................. 114
PART VI ................................................................................... 118
GLOBAL CASE STUDIES .................................................... 119
Chapter 24 ............................................................................... 120
CASE STUDY 1 ...................................................................... 121
CASE STUDY 3 ...................................................................... 124
CASE STUDY 4 ...................................................................... 125
PART VII ................................................................................. 126

CONCLUSION & ADDITIONAL RESOURCES ............... 127
CONCLUSION .......................................................................... 128
BIBLIOGRAPHY ..................................................................... 130

To all the mentors worldwide who have selflessly invested their time, wisdom, and care in guiding and nurturing me. Your unwavering support, genuine interest, and invaluable teachings have shaped and still shaped my journey and profoundly enriched my life. This book is dedicated to you, with heartfelt gratitude and appreciation for the profound impact you've had on my personal and professional growth.

# THE MENTOR & THE MENTEE

A Roadmap for Growth

**PATIENCE SAKUTUKWA**

# THE MENTOR & THE MENTEE

A Roadmap for Growth

**PATIENCE SAKUTUKWA**

Copyright ©2024 @Patience Sakutukwa
**All rights reserved.**

No part of this book may be reproduced or transmitted in any form or by any means, electronic or mechanical, including photocopying, recording, or by any information storage and retrieval system, without permission in writing from the copyright owner.

ISBN: 978-0-7961-7323-2

Edited by Bethel Publishing House
Layout by Bethel Publishing House
Cover Design by Bright Chinyerem
Published at Bethel Publishing House
Printed in South Africa

Bethel Publishing House

# EPIGRAPHY

*"If you are planting for a year, plant grain. If you are planting for a decade, plant trees. If you are planting for a century, plant people."* -The Chinese Proverb

# DEDICATION

To all the mentors around the world who have selflessly invested their time, wisdom, and care in guiding and nurturing me. Your unwavering support, genuine interest, and invaluable teachings have shaped and still shaped my journey and enriched my life in profound ways. This book is dedicated to you, with heartfelt gratitude and appreciation for the profound impact you've had on my personal and professional growth.

# ACKNOWLEDGMENTS

Writing this book has been a deeply personal journey, and I am profoundly grateful to all those who have supported and inspired me along the way. First and foremost, I would like to express my heartfelt gratitude to my, my uncle and aunties, my Pastors, my mentors, whose guidance, wisdom, and unwavering support have shaped my personal and professional development in profound ways. Your belief in me and your willingness to invest your time and energy in my growth has been valuable, and I am forever grateful for the impact you have had on my life. I would also like to extend my appreciation to my mentees, whose curiosity, enthusiasm, and fresh perspectives have challenged me to grow and learn as a mentor. Your willingness to trust me with your aspirations and struggles has been a humbling privilege, and I am honored to have been a part of your journey. Additionally, I would like to thank my family and friends for their unwavering encouragement and support throughout the writing process.

Your belief in me has been a constant source of inspiration, and I am grateful for your patience, understanding, and love. Finally, I would like to express my gratitude to the readers of this book. It is my sincere hope that the insights and reflections shared within these pages will resonate with you and empower you to embrace the transformative potential of mentorship in your own life.

# FOREWORD

Mentoring someone is not just a duty; it is a burden, a responsibility, and a calling. The true measure of your success in life lies in the legacy you leave behind the works that outlive you. One day, as I prayed, God spoke to me, saying, "In ministry, your greatest impact is not in what you do, but in who you raise." When God grants you the grace to mentor a person, take it as an honor, for He has entrusted you with a future generation. As a mentee blessed with the opportunity to learn and draw from deep wells of wisdom, be grateful, and never harm the source that once nourished you. As you read this phenomenal book by Prophetess Patience Sakutukwa, keep your spirit open to receive its life-enriching and empowering messages for both your journey and ministry. There is no perfect mentor in this world, but when God gives you the privilege to sit at someone's feet, stay focused, and understand why He sent you there.

Apostle Believe Tanaka Isaac
Presiding Founder of Ramah Ministries
Legal Advisor & Advocate

# PREFACE

In the bustling landscape of personal professional and spiritual development, few relationships hold as much transformative power as mentorship. It's a dynamic interplay of guidance, support, and shared wisdom, where both mentor and mentee embark on a journey of growth and discovery. As I reflect on my own experiences as both a mentor and a mentee, I'm struck by the profound impact these relationships have had on shaping my path, illuminating the way forward, and sometimes, even challenging my assumptions. I have found myself battling with the area of mentorship and yet it's one of the things I have pursued in my life more than anything. I realized I did not know much of it and also that what I knew was not it all. Apart from therapy in my writings, I have developed a way to hear from God clearly to a point I feel there is some mentorship that God wants to do in me and you. So I am committing to just be a vessel and serve as a mentee. In this book, "The Mentor and the Mentee," I delve into the intricacies of mentorship, drawing from my successes, failures, and lessons learned along the way.

Through personal anecdotes, practical insights, and thoughtful reflections, I aim to offer guidance to both mentors and mentees navigating their own mentorship journeys. From defining the essence of mentorship to navigating challenges and envisioning the future, this book is a testament to the enduring power of mentorship in transforming lives and driving positive change. Whether you're a seasoned mentor, a hopeful mentee, or someone curious about the dynamics of mentorship, I invite you to embark on this journey with me. May the pages that follow inspire you, challenge you, and ultimately, empower you to embrace the transformative potential of mentorship in your own life and the lives of those around you.

# PART I

# UNDERSTANDING MENTORSHIP

# INTRODUCTION

Before I could read or write, my mother taught me the most profound lesson of all: to live as though I am always seen, not by man, but by God. This understanding came not from a formal classroom but from the intimate setting of our home, where my mother's mentorship unfolded in the simplest yet most profound ways.

I can still see her in my mind, bent over the basin by the outdoor tap, water running steadily as she scrubbed clothes with rhythmic precision. Around her, buckets stood in neat rows one for soapy water, another for rinsing, and one waiting for wringing. The morning sun cast a warm glow, and the steady sound of running water filled the air. My mother my first mentor, my earliest guide introduced me to God in this simple, everyday moment. "Mwari havazvifarire," she said, her voice firm yet patient as she caught me wasting water by the tap. God does not like this. I froze, water dripping from my small hands, my heart racing with curiosity. Her words stirred something within me. Who was this Mwari, and why did He care about the water I was playing with?

"Mwari ndiani?" I asked, my childlike curiosity overpowering my hesitation. Who is God?

She paused, her hands resting briefly on a shirt she was scrubbing.

Her tired eyes lifted to meet mine for a fleeting moment before she looked up at the sky. "Anokuona," she said simply, pointing upward. He sees you.

I followed her finger, my gaze fixed on the endless blue sky above us. "Kuonei?" I asked, determined to understand. Seeing what?

She sighed, dipping the shirt into the soapy water again. "Zvese," she replied matter-of-factly. Everything.

That single word left me in awe. My young imagination sprang to life, constructing an image of God.

## PATIENCE SAKUTUKWA

I pictured Him as a wise, grandfatherly figure, dressed in a sky-blue short-sleeved shirt and a royal blue sun hat perhaps inspired by the colors of my school uniform. In my mind, He was always watching, always present.

"Anondiona?" I asked hesitantly, my voice trembling with guilt. Does He see me? She nodded, wringing out the shirt as water splashed onto the ground. "Anokuona kunyange paunoba shuga yangu," she added, her tone steady but piercing. He sees you even when you steal my sugar. I froze, the memory of sneaking spoonfuls of sugar from her small silver sugar basin rushing back. I had thought myself clever, smuggling the sweet crystals while no one was watching. But the idea that God had seen every spoonful sent a chill down my spine. I glanced at the sugar basin in the corner of my mind, almost tasting the guilt. To this day, I don't enjoy sweet things not even on my birthdays. Cakes and sugary treats hold little appeal. It feels as though her words "Mwari vanoranga" (God punishes) have lingered with me, shaping my choices in ways I didn't fully understand until later.

As I stood there by the tap, I reached for the water again, unable to resist the cool splash. The tap flowed freely in my small hands until her voice broke through again. "Ndakuudza kuti Mwari havazvifarire," she said, this time with an unmistakable sharpness.

I told you, God does not like it. I pulled back quickly, the weight of her words heavy on my young heart. That day, I felt the full force of a conscience shaped not by human judgment but by the omnipresent gaze of God.

My mother, without realizing it, had introduced me to the profound concept of accountability living as though I was always seen, even when no one else was watching. This was my first experience with mentorship. It was not a formal lesson or a structured teaching but a moment rooted in love, guidance, and example. My mother's words and actions left an indelible mark on my soul, instilling in me a reverence for God that continues to guide me. As I reflect on that moment, I see how mentorship begins in the simplest of settings by the tap, amidst splashes of water, and in the quiet conversations that shape who we become.

It is this understanding of mentorship that I hope to share with you in the pages that follow. What I didn't realize at the time was how deeply my mother took me seriously, even at such a young age. She paid attention to the smallest things I said, treating my words with an importance that I didn't fully understand then.

Perhaps it was my curiosity about Mwari, or maybe it was her natural instinct to guide us, but she made it her mission to nurture not just our minds but also our spirits. Every evening before we went to bed, my younger sister and I had a special task: to memorize Bible verses she taught us. My mother would sit firmly on her bed, her treasured Shona Bible open in her hands, while we sat on the floor before her. Strict as she was about her bedding, she never allowed our dirty legs to mess it. Even in her discipline, there was love and order. With the same authority and care that defined her, she would read aloud scriptures that would later become the foundation of my faith. John 1:12: *"But to all who received Him, who believed in His name, He gave the right to become children of God."* John 3:16: *"For God so loved the world that He gave His only Son, that whoever believes in Him should not perish but have eternal life."*

Psalms 14:1: *"The fool says in his heart, 'There is no God.'"* Revelation 1:7: *"Behold, He is coming with the clouds, and every eye will see Him..."* These scriptures became a nightly ritual, her voice repeating them over and over until they were etched in our young minds.

"Recite them," she would instruct, her tone firm yet encouraging. We would stumble at first, but with her patient persistence, we soon mastered them. She didn't rest until we could recite the verses perfectly even in our sleep. At times she would pinch our ears until we mastered those scriptures. Beyond teaching us scripture, she introduced us to the beauty of Bible stories. One that stood out to me was the story of

## PATIENCE SAKUTUKWA

Joseph and his dreams in Genesis 37. It fascinated me a young man whose dreams carried the weight of destiny. I remember being so captivated by Joseph's story that I purchased a book about him during one of our school book sales. My mother always supported me whenever these sales came around, making sure I could buy small Bibles and books about Daniel, Moses, and other great biblical figures.

Moses' story remains especially vivid. My mother didn't just narrate it; she brought it to life. I can still hear Charles Charamba's song about Moses and the Israelites playing in the background as she told us the tale of their deliverance. It was more than a story it was a lesson in faith, resilience, and the power of God's hand at work. I will never forget her narration about the 10 Plagues and the rebellious Pharaoh.

We were attending Pentecostal Assemblies of God Church and she made sure we participated in the Sunday school activities such as drama, bible recitations, and many more. This gave me a firm foundation of Who God Is and His unconditional Love. My mother might not have left me anything tangible, as my father did, but she left me something far greater, JESUS. She gave me the greatest gift, one that has no expiry date, no conditions, and no limits: Jesus Christ. A gift so eternal and profound that it continues to sustain me to this day. Where her guidance left off, His covering has remained steadfast. These memories, scattered across the years like pieces of a jigsaw puzzle, are now coming together, forming a picture of the woman who shaped so much of who I am.

Over 30 years later, I see her motherly skills with such clarity. She had an instinctive ability to mentor, to guide, to nurture in ways that leave me in awe. If I were to have children of my own one day, I know I would struggle to match her level of parental mentorship. As I planned this book, these sacred moments came flooding back to me. I see now how my mother's love for God was her greatest gift to us.

She poured that love into her children, guiding us to know Him, fear Him, and trust Him. Mum, you will forever be loved and missed.

# THE MENTOR & THE MENTEE

Thank you for taking me seriously, for nurturing me in faith, and for teaching me what it means to live for God. Your lessons are eternal, shaping my life and my journey in ways I will never stop cherishing. I remember vividly the day of my mother's funeral. Among the many words spoken, one line stood out to me and has stayed with me all these years: *"Evelyn finished the work."* It was a profound statement, spoken by someone who recognized the completeness of her efforts in raising my sister and me. At the time, I didn't fully grasp its depth, but looking back now, it makes so much sense. They were referring to the skills my mother had instilled in us at such a young age the ability to wash our undergarments and clothes with care, and even to cook *sadza* on a high stove. These tasks, though simple, were not common for children of the age I was in, yet my mother had ensured we could manage them. She had equipped us not just for survival, but for independence and responsibility. Her funeral was the first one where I truly understood what it meant to lose someone.

I felt the weight of it deeply that day. It was more than the absence of her presence; it was the realization of the void her passing left in my life. Yet, hearing those words, *"Evelyn finished the work"* gave me a sense of comfort. My mother may not have been there to witness all the stages of our growth, but she had laid the foundation. She had prepared her girls for life in a way that only a mother with a purposeful heart could. And as much as her absence hurt, I now see that her work was indeed finished. She had poured everything she could into us, leaving behind a legacy of strength, resilience, and faith. Many claim to understand mentorship today, boasting about their roles as mentors or mentees.

They flaunt their eloquence and the numerous groups eager to learn from them, yet there are often no tangible results to demonstrate their effectiveness. The word "mentor" has lost weight; many aspire to it, but few possess the true capacity. Pride often stands in the way of those who desire mentorship, while some mentor individuals who should be mentoring them.

True mentorship is a delicate balance of guidance and empowerment, like the proverb, "Give a man a fish, and you feed him for a day; teach a man to fish, and you feed him for a lifetime." It equips the mentee with the tools to navigate their path, fostering independence and growth.

Consider the biblical example of Moses mentoring Joshua, preparing him to lead the Israelites into the Promised Land after Moses' death. As the scripture says, "The LORD would speak to Moses face to face, as one speaks to a friend. Then Moses would return to the camp, but his young aide Joshua son of Nun did not leave the tent" (Exodus 33:11). This relationship exemplifies the depth of commitment and the transfer of wisdom that true mentorship entails.

Similarly, the prophet Elijah mentored Elisha, who would succeed him as a prophet in Israel. Their relationship is captured in Elijah's query to Elisha: "Let me inherit a double portion of your spirit," to which Elijah responds, "If you see me when I am taken from you, it will be yours otherwise, it will not" (2 Kings 2:9). This interaction highlights the aspirational nature of mentorship and the profound influence a mentor can have on their mentee's journey.

Paul mentored Timothy, guiding him in his role as a young church leader, urging him to "fan into flame the gift of God" (2 Timothy 1:6). Naomi, Ruth's mother-in-law, mentored her in navigating life after their husbands' deaths. Ruth's declaration, "Where you go I will go, and where you stay I will stay" (Ruth 1:16), reflects the profound personal and emotional support integral to effective mentorship. Throughout history, notable mentorships have shaped lives and legacies. Jethro mentored Moses, Elijah mentored Elisha, and Jesus mentored the 12 Apostles, who in turn mentored many others.

There is wisdom in the Chinese proverb, *"If you are planting for a year, plant grain. If you are planting for a decade, plant trees. If you are planting for a century, plant people."* Ron Lee Davis captures the essence of mentorship: "The deepest dimensions of Christian life cannot simply be taught in a classroom or a book. To be proven and assimilated, Christian life must be heard, seen, felt, studied intently, handled, lived, and experienced."

*"The best way to predict your child's future is to create it."* - Abraham Lincoln. Parental mentorship is a sacred and transformative relationship that shapes the lives and destinies of future generations. Mentors in this realm, often parents themselves, provide guidance, support, and unconditional love to help children navigate the challenges of growing up and become the best versions of themselves. From teaching life skills to imparting moral values, parental mentors play a pivotal role in shaping the character, values, and beliefs of their children. Through their example and guidance, they instill confidence, resilience, and a sense of purpose in their children, empowering them to navigate life's ups and downs with grace and integrity.

# Chapter 1

# The Importance of Mentorship

*"The delicate balance of mentoring someone is not creating them in your image, but allowing them to create themselves."* – Steven Spielberg

After losing our parents, my younger sister and I were entrusted to the care of my uncle and aunt, my father's elder brother, and his wife. Their home became a sanctuary for us, a place where love and discipline intertwined to shape our futures. My uncle, a man of unwavering integrity, had an immense and positive influence on my life. His commitment to his faith and family became a beacon of hope during a time of profound loss. It was an unexpected joy to discover that their family attended the Assemblies of God Church. The vibrant community felt both familiar and refreshingly new. I quickly found my footing, immersing myself in service and embracing the opportunity to grow spiritually. My uncle, who remains an elder in the church, was deeply involved in hosting crusades with *Africa Back to God Missions*.

His strict yet principled nature instilled values of accountability and dedication in me, values that have echoed throughout my life and ministry. As I reflect on my theological studies today, it amazes me how the seeds sown during those formative years continue to flourish. One of my key modules is Missions and Church Planting, a calling that was subtly nurtured by my uncle's example. Meanwhile, my grandmother, an Anglican elder, contributed to my spiritual formation in her own unique way. She would call upon me to deliver short sermons, sing alongside my sisters, or act in church dramas during events and camps. One such event, the annual Bernard Mizeki celebration, left an indelible mark on my heart. Bernard Mizeki's story of faith, courage, and sacrifice resonated deeply. As a missionary to the Shona people in Zimbabwe, his martyrdom in 1896 became a powerful testament to the cost of faith and the calling to spread the gospel. For me, these celebrations were more than mere traditions. They were a vivid reminder of what it means to live and die for Christ. My family's mentorship extended beyond structured activities. My elder sisters nurtured my love for worship, often guiding me through melodies that touched the soul.

My cousins trusted me with their deepest confidences, teaching me the importance of empathy and listening. These experiences, woven together, became the bedrock of my theological understanding and ministry.

Looking back, I realize how mentorship shaped every facet of my being, long before I could fully comprehend its significance. It is disheartening to see how mentorship in today's society often feels transactional, stripped of the genuine care and guidance it once embodied. Christian author Eugene Peterson observed, "We are made for God; every detail of our lives is crafted in reference to him." This profound truth reminds us that mentorship, at its core, is not merely about imparting knowledge but about shaping hearts through discipleship. John Stott beautifully expressed this when he wrote, "Discipleship means identity with Christ and participation in his sufferings, mission, and glory."

My uncle, my grandmother, and my family lived out this truth, embodying a mentorship that extended beyond words into actions that spoke louder than any sermon. Their guidance reminds me that mentorship is not a path to conformity but an avenue for transformation.

True mentorship is about enabling others to discover their unique potential and navigate life's challenges with courage and faith. It is not about replicating ourselves but about empowering others to refine their gifts and purpose. As I look to the future, I feel a deep responsibility to pay this forward, to mentor others as I was mentored, and to restore the sacredness of this timeless practice.

Mentorship serves as a guiding force in personal and professional growth, offering support, encouragement, and wisdom to help us navigate life's complexities. From ancient times to modern societies, mentorship has been pivotal in passing down knowledge, traditions, and values, ensuring humanity's progress. At its heart, mentorship is about relationships rooted in trust, respect, and mutual understanding. It is a bond that transcends generations, empowering individuals to overcome obstacles and realize their dreams. The impact of mentorship is profound. It creates a culture of learning and collaboration that enriches not just individuals but entire communities. It fosters a legacy of wisdom, compassion, and hope that transcends time.

By investing in mentorship, we create a ripple effect of positive change, paving the way for future generations to thrive. Imagine this book as a journey we embark on together, much like a road trip to an unfamiliar destination. Each chapter will be a milestone, each page a step closer to a place of fulfilled dreams and divine purpose. Along the way, we will encounter challenges, seek guidance, and celebrate victories. Like a road trip, mentorship is not just about the destination but about the experiences, lessons, and connections we gather along the way. As I write these words, I am reminded of the countless hands that shaped me, mentors who saw potential in me even when I could not. Their legacy calls me to action, to mentor others with the same selfless love and dedication.

By embracing the transformative power of mentorship, we honor those who guided us and leave a legacy that inspires others to follow.

# Chapter 2

# Effects of Mentorship

*"Mentoring is a brain to pick, an ear to listen, and a push in the right direction."* -John Crosby

Over the past years, I have been mentored by the great when I did not know how to define this setup. I was privileged enough to get mentorship from Sunday schools where my biblical skills and moral values were harnessed. My mother was the first to introduce me to God. My two grandmothers are heroes of faith and prayer warriors. My uncle is a man of integrity and constant faith. Sometimes they did not need to sit me down and talk but they lived and lived their talk. I cannot explain how effective mentorship is without involving my experiences. I have been privileged to get great mentors in different seasons. My grandfather taught me how to cook sadza (pap) without leaking it from the pot.

My understanding of mentorship began in 2008 when I had the privilege to learn from one of my resident Pastor who took her time to invest in my spiritual and mental wellness. She also created time to pray with me every morning I would visit for weekends at her house and sometimes she would take me for drives. She inspired me as a woman in ministry and made me believe that if a woman can birth Jesus, she can preach to him too. I also had powerful guidance in some Apostles, Prophets, Evangelists and Teachers who nurtured my prayer life and word digestion. I felt like I had not read the bible before in their teachings and prayer sessions. It has been not a rosy road for me to be constantly being mentored but I am forever grateful to have such a voice in my life. From a distance, I have been privileged to encounter Fathers and Mothers of Faith and of them and most of these have honored me with their access in a humble way. The beginnings of mentorship, when executed effectively, has the power to shape destinies and transform lives. Throughout history, icons and visionaries have risen to greatness with the guiding hand of a mentor.

# PATIENCE SAKUTUKWA

Consider the relationship between Socrates and Plato, where the wisdom of the former ignited the philosophical brilliance of the latter, laying the groundwork for Western philosophy as we know it today. Or reflect on the mentorship between Martin Luther King Jr. and Mahatma Gandhi, whose shared principles of nonviolent resistance reverberated across continents, inspiring movements for civil rights and social justice. In the realm of business, the impact of mentorship is equally profound. Silicon Valley legends like Steve Jobs and Mark Zuckerberg credit their success in part to the guidance of seasoned mentors who provided invaluable insights and strategic counsel. These visionary leaders didn't just create companies; they revolutionized entire industries, leaving an indelible mark on the world.

Beyond individual success stories, mentorship has catalyzed advancements in various fields, from science and technology to the arts and humanities. Consider the mentorship of Marie Curie, whose groundbreaking research in radioactivity laid the foundation for modern nuclear physics and earned her two Nobel Prizes. Her mentorship of future Nobel laureates, such as her daughter Irène Joliot-Curie, continued to drive scientific innovation for generations to come.

In the world of sports, mentorship plays a pivotal role in cultivating champions. Legendary basketball coach John Wooden mentored players like Kareem Abdul-Jabbar and Bill Walton, instilling in them not just athletic prowess but also principles of discipline, teamwork, and integrity. The ripple effects of his mentorship extended far beyond the basketball court, shaping the character and leadership of his players long after their playing days were over. Anna was eager to advance in her career and sought out a mentor in her field. She found someone who seemed successful and well-connected and eagerly accepted their guidance. However, as time went on, Anna realized that her mentor's advice was leading her down a path that didn't align with her passions or values.

## THE MENTOR & THE MENTEE

Despite her misgivings, Anna continued to follow her mentor's directives, fearing that she would miss out on valuable opportunities if she didn't comply. Eventually, Anna found herself feeling unfulfilled and disillusioned, realizing too late that she had allowed herself to be led astray by the wrong mentor. In the pursuit of mentorship, many individuals abandon their authentic selves in an attempt to fit in.

They fall into line, adopting behaviors and language that conform to societal expectations, even if it means repressing their true identities. This assimilation, while sometimes seen as a strategy for survival, can lead to inner conflict and a sense of fulfillment. The rage that arises from suppressing one's true identity is real, as is the desperate need for release. Effective mentors wear many hats. They are teachers, advisors, and confidants. They offer a roadmap to success, helping mentees avoid common pitfalls and seize opportunities. In the professional realm, mentors guide their mentees through the labyrinth of corporate structures and career advancements.

Mentorship, as defined by dictionaries and academic discourse, is the dynamic relationship between a mentor, an experienced and wise guide, and a mentee, a receptive learner seeking growth and development. However, its roots delve deeper, echoing the profound mentor-mentee relationships found throughout history, particularly within the pages of sacred texts. Mentorship has been an integral part of spiritual and theological development throughout history.

Just as in other realms of life, effective mentorship within the Christian tradition has shaped destinies, transformed lives, and advanced the spread of faith. Consider the mentorship of St. Augustine by St. Ambrose, which played a pivotal role in Augustine's conversion to Christianity and subsequent contributions to theology. Augustine's writings, influenced by his mentorship, continue to shape Christian thought and doctrine to this day. Similarly, the Desert Fathers and

## PATIENCE SAKUTUKWA

Mothers of the early Christian church served as spiritual mentors to countless believers seeking guidance in their faith journeys. These ascetic pioneers withdrew from society to live lives of prayer, contemplation, and simplicity, serving as examples of devotion and holiness to those who sought their counsel.

In more recent times, spiritual Christian mentors like Dietrich Bonhoeffer have exemplified the power of mentorship in times of adversity. Bonhoeffer, a Lutheran pastor and theologian, mentored seminarians and resistance fighters in Nazi Germany, challenging them to live out their faith courageously in the face of tyranny. His mentorship inspired countless individuals to resist injustice and uphold the values of compassion, justice, and solidarity.

Additionally, charismatic mentors have played a significant role in theological development, particularly in the charismatic movement within Christianity. These mentors, often with dynamic personalities and spiritual gifts, have mentored individuals in the practice of spiritual gifts, prophetic ministry, and fervent prayer. Their mentorship has empowered believers to embrace their spiritual identity and engage in transformative ministry. Beyond the realm of faith, academia has long recognized the significance of mentorship in personal and professional development. Scholars such as Daniel Levinson and Jeanne Nakamura have explored the multifaceted nature of mentorship, highlighting its role in identity formation, skill acquisition, and career advancement. Drawing from psychological theories and empirical research, academia illuminates the intricate dynamics at play within mentor-mentee relationships. While mentorship offers tremendous benefits, including personal growth, skill development, and professional advancement, it also carries inherent dangers. Unbalanced power dynamics, unrealistic expectations, and the risk of dependency are among the pitfalls that both mentors and mentees must navigate with care.

# Chapter 3

# Signs That You Need a Mentor

*"Our chief want in life is somebody who will make us do what we can."*
-Ralph Waldo Emerson

In the grand mosaic of personal and professional development, there comes a moment when the threads of one's journey begin to fray, revealing gaps that can only be mended by the guidance of a mentor. The ancient proverb, "He who asks a question remains a fool for five minutes; he who does not ask remains a fool forever," underscores the importance of seeking wisdom. When you find yourself at a crossroads, unsure of which path to tread, it may be a sign that you need a mentor. Feelings of stagnation, a lack of direction, and the overwhelming weight of uncharted territories are all indicators. The role of a mentor is akin to that of a lighthouse, providing illumination and direction during a storm.

One of the key signs that you need a mentor is feeling stuck in your current situation. Whether in your career or personal life, if you find yourself facing the same obstacles without making progress, a mentor can provide the fresh perspective and strategic advice needed to move forward. There are times when I have felt stuck, when I longed to pray but couldn't, or when I wanted to start a new project only to find myself trapped by uncertainty. These moments were my wake-up call, urging me to seek counsel. I realized that embracing guidance from others could unlock new possibilities. A mentor brings clarity, helping you identify the root of the issue and guiding you toward a path that may have previously seemed unclear.

Similarly, a lack of direction is a strong indicator that mentorship could be beneficial. If you are uncertain about your goals or the steps required to achieve them, a mentor can help you clarify your vision and create a roadmap for success. I've experienced periods in my journey when the way forward seemed foggy, and it wasn't until I opened myself to the advice and counsel of others that I found the direction I needed.

Learning from those ahead of you, from those who inspire and challenge you, can make all the difference. The clarity that comes from a mentor's insight has the power to transform ambiguity into a focused drive. Another sign is the overwhelming weight of uncharted territories. Entering a new field or taking on a challenging project can be daunting. A mentor with experience in that area can guide you through the unknown, helping you avoid common pitfalls and capitalize on opportunities. I have often felt the burden of stepping into new territories whether in ministry or personal projects feeling as though I was treading unfamiliar ground. In those moments, a mentor's wisdom helped me navigate these challenges with more confidence, knowing that I was not alone in the journey. Moreover, if you lack confidence in your decisions or frequently second-guess yourself, a mentor can provide the reassurance and validation needed to build self-assurance and decisiveness. In my own experience, there have been times when I've been paralyzed by doubt, unsure whether I was making the right choice. But the steady guidance of someone who has walked the path before me has been invaluable in reinforcing my confidence and encouraging me to move forward boldly.

Mentors offer not just wisdom but emotional support, helping you navigate the highs and lows of your journey with encouragement and a steady presence. At times, we may feel isolated, lacking a support system or someone to confide in. This is another indicator that mentorship could be beneficial. Having someone to listen, offer advice, or provide a different perspective can make all the difference when we face difficult decisions or moments of uncertainty. I have often turned to trusted mentors, not only for professional advice but also for emotional support, particularly in challenging times when I needed reassurance and a sounding board. Their presence helped me stay grounded and focused on the bigger picture, reminding me that I was not walking my path alone.

Recognizing the signs that indicate the need for mentorship is the first step toward embarking on a transformative journey of growth and development. Sometimes, it's not easy to acknowledge our own limitations or areas where we can improve. However, these signs serve as gentle nudges, urging us to seek guidance and support from those who have walked the path before us.

Perhaps you find yourself facing recurring challenges or obstacles in your personal or professional life, unsure of how to overcome them. Maybe you feel stuck in a rut, lacking the clarity or direction needed to pursue your goals and aspirations. Or it could be that you're yearning for someone to offer insights, wisdom, and perspective that can illuminate your path and empower you to reach new heights.

In any case, these signs are not meant to be seen as weaknesses but as opportunities for growth and learning. Embracing the idea of mentorship means embracing vulnerability, humility, and a willingness to embark on a journey of self-discovery and self-improvement. It's about recognizing that we all have areas where we can grow and flourish, and that seeking guidance from a mentor is a courageous step toward unlocking our full potential. As I reflect on my own journey, I've learned that mentorship is not just about receiving advice; it's about learning to embrace the wisdom of others and using it to propel yourself forward with renewed purpose and clarity.

# Chapter 4

# Signs That You Are a Mentor

*"A mentor empowers a person to see a possible future, and believe it can be obtained."* - Shawn Hitchcock

As you navigate your journey of growth and development, you may find yourself embodying qualities and characteristics that make you a natural mentor to others. These signs serve as affirmations of your ability to inspire, guide, and empower those around you, whether in your personal or professional sphere. Perhaps you notice that people often come to you for advice, seeking your insights and wisdom on matters close to their hearts. Your words carry weight, resonating deeply with those who seek your counsel, like an echo across the canyons of their minds, inspiring them to strive for greatness. Maybe you find joy in sharing your experiences, knowledge, and expertise with others.

Like a gardener tending to the seeds of wisdom, nurturing them with care until they blossom into vibrant flowers of understanding. Your willingness to share your journey, with all its ups and downs, serves as a roadmap for others traversing similar paths, guiding them through the twists and turns of life's labyrinth. Reflecting on the twists and turns of my own journey, I've come to understand that mentorship is not always a deliberate endeavor; rather, it often emerges organically, fueled by an earnest desire to uplift and empower others. Over the years, I've been humbled by a deluge of requests for guidance and mentorship, spanning a diverse spectrum of individuals from aspiring professionals to seasoned government officials, each seeking solace and direction in their personal and professional lives. Initially, I never fancied myself a mentor, seeing my own journey as a perpetual quest for growth and enlightenment. However, as I engaged with these seekers of wisdom, I gradually unearthed a latent capacity within myself to nurture and inspire those who crossed my path.

# THE MENTOR & THE MENTEE

You may attempt to evade it, but the allure of mentorship has an uncanny knack for finding its way back to you, no matter where you roam. In the rich tapestry of human interactions, there exists a cadre of individuals whose very presence acts as a beacon, igniting sparks of inspiration and stoking fires of ambition in those fortunate enough to cross their paths. These individuals, often unbeknownst to themselves, possess an innate quality a blend of wisdom, empathy, and authenticity that marks them as mentors, guides, and champions of growth. As you traverse the journey of life, here are telltale signs that you may indeed be one of these luminaries, shaping destinies and unleashing greatness in those around you. Maya, a radiant beacon of warmth and sagacity, possessed an irresistible magnetism that naturally drew others towards her, despite her reluctance to claim the mantle of leadership. In the bustling corridors of her workplace, Maya found herself inundated with colleagues seeking her counsel on matters both personal and professional. When she took the stage at a local event, her words flowed with a grace and eloquence that captivated hearts and minds alike.

Her message of resilience and hope struck a resonant chord, inspiring listeners to harness their inner strength and pursue their dreams with unwavering resolve. Little did Maya realize that her unwitting mentorship would ripple outward, touching lives in ways she could scarcely imagine. Perhaps it's your natural gift for listening, empathizing, and offering support to those in need that sets you apart, like a lighthouse cutting through the darkness, guiding lost ships safely to harbor. Your compassionate ear and open heart provide solace to those weathering life's storms, offering them a beacon of hope in their darkest hours.

Mentors possess an uncanny knack for identifying the unique talents and gifts that lie dormant within their mentees. They nurture these seeds of potential with tender care, encouraging their charges to venture beyond the confines of their comfort zones and embrace the pursuit of excellence. Through the creation of opportunities, the forging of connections, and the embodiment of exemplary lifestyles, mentors inspire greatness in those they guide, leaving an indelible mark on the tapestry of human potential.

Alex, a born leader who shied away from the limelight, initially balked at the notion of assuming a mentorship role when approached by a colleague. Plagued by self-doubt and uncertainty about his qualifications, Alex hesitated to embrace the opportunity. Yet, upon deeper reflection, he recognized the transformative potential of guiding others towards their goals. With newfound determination coursing through his veins, Alex embarked on his mentorship journey, his initial reservations melting away in the face of his unwavering commitment to empowering those around him. What began as a tentative acceptance of mentorship soon blossomed into a fervent crusade for upliftment and empowerment, as Alex discovered the boundless impact he could wield on the lives of others.

In any case, these signs are not meant to be seen as burdens but rather as blessings that affirm your purpose and calling as a mentor. Embracing the role of a mentor means embracing responsibility, compassion, and a commitment to nurturing the growth and development of others. It's about recognizing that your journey is not just about personal success but also about lifting others up and helping them shine brightly in their own right.

Mentorship often begins with an inner calling, a desire to share knowledge and experiences with others. You may be a mentor if you find that people frequently seek your advice and value your insights. This inclination to guide others, coupled with a wealth of knowledge and experience, positions you as a mentor. A good teacher is like a candle; it consumes itself to light the way for others, aptly describing the selfless nature of mentorship. One of the signs that you are a mentor is the ability to inspire and motivate others. If your words and actions resonate deeply with those around you, encouraging them to strive for

## THE MENTOR & THE MENTEE

their best, you possess a key quality of a mentor. Additionally, if you derive satisfaction from seeing others succeed and grow, this indicates a natural mentoring spirit. Another sign is the willingness to listen and empathize.

## PATIENCE SAKUTUKWA

Effective mentors are not just providers of advice; they are also attentive listeners who understand their mentees' challenges and aspirations. This empathy allows mentors to offer tailored guidance that addresses the mentee's unique needs. If you find joy in nurturing growth and have the patience to guide others through their journeys, these are strong indicators that you are meant to be a mentor. Mentors also exhibit a deep commitment to their own continuous learning and development. They recognize that the journey of growth never truly ends, and they lead by example, showing their mentees the importance of lifelong learning. If you are passionate about self-improvement and are eager to share your journey with others, you have the qualities of an effective mentor.

# Chapter 5

# Identifying Your Mentor

*"When the student is ready, the teacher will appear."* – Unknown
Identifying the right mentor is a pivotal step in personal and professional growth. A mentor is not just a guide, but a key to unlocking your potential. They offer unique insights, experiences, and perspectives that can profoundly influence your journey. Whether you're navigating your career, relationships, or personal development, choosing the right mentor can accelerate your progress. But how do you identify a mentor who truly adds value to your life?

Mentorship is a deeply personal journey, and no two mentor-mentee relationships are alike. As you embark on your quest to find a mentor, it's important to first define your needs and goals. What do you want to achieve? What qualities in a mentor will empower you to get there?

Exploring mentorship styles and reflecting on your own aspirations will lay the foundation for this transformative journey.

## Understanding Mentorship Styles

Mentorship comes in various forms. Some mentors are sage advisors, offering wisdom and guidance based on their years of experience. Others may be more compassionate listeners, providing emotional support and a safe space for vulnerability. Each mentorship style has its place in your growth journey, and it's important to identify which resonates most with you.

## Qualities to Look for in a Mentor

First and foremost, a mentor should be someone you respect and admire. Their values should align with yours, and they should embody the principles you hold dear. Look for individuals who have achieved success in areas where you aspire to grow.

Whose expertise in those fields can help guide you on your own path. A credible mentor demonstrates experience, knowledge, and a genuine commitment to fostering the growth of others. Accessibility and approachability are also crucial factors. A good mentor's door should always be open, inviting dialogue and exchange. The relationship should foster openness and honesty, allowing for meaningful conversations where you can express your challenges and ambitions without fear of judgment. Constructive feedback is also essential mentorship thrives when trust and communication are nurtured.

## Sarah's Journey: A Lesson in Discernment

Sarah's story is a powerful example of how easy it is to be misled when selecting a mentor. In her search for guidance, she found herself drawn to individuals who seemed outwardly successful. However, she learned the hard way that charisma does not always equate to true mentorship.

Many of the people she trusted did not have her best interests at heart, and she often found herself disappointed and disillusioned. However, Sarah's journey also reveals an important lesson: sometimes, the most effective mentors are not the ones who stand out the most. One of her colleagues, a quiet and humble individual, had been offering guidance all along—guidance Sarah had initially overlooked. It wasn't until Sarah faced a series of setbacks and reflected on her mistakes that she recognized the value of this humble mentor. In her darkest hour, she turned to this colleague, realizing that the guidance she had rejected was the very support she needed.

## The Importance of Proper Mentorship Selection

My own journey mirrors Sarah's, and it has taught me the importance of careful discernment when choosing mentors. Many times, I hastily sought guidance from so-called mentors without truly understanding their backgrounds or assessing whether they had the tools to help me achieve my goals.

This lack of insight led to delays in my personal growth, my academic pursuits, and my professional development. The failure to identify the right mentor can be a major roadblock. I've learned that it's essential to not only consider a mentor's qualifications but also their values and intentions. The wrong mentor can lead you down the wrong path, whereas the right one can help you navigate the storms of life.

## Navigating the Mentor-Mentee Journey

Finding the right mentor requires more than just seeking someone with the right credentials. It involves identifying someone whose values align with yours and who is genuinely interested in your growth. Here are a few key factors to keep in mind:

1. **Alignment of Values**: A strong mentor-mentee relationship is built on shared principles. If a mentor's values resonate with yours, it will be easier to build mutual respect and trust.

2. **Experience and Expertise**: Look for mentors who have walked the path you wish to follow.

Their insights, shaped by their experiences, can help you avoid common mistakes and navigate challenges.

3. **Approachability and Communication**: A good mentor is someone who makes you feel comfortable. Open communication is vital for effective mentorship, allowing you to share your challenges and aspirations without hesitation.

4. **Commitment to Your Growth**: Choose a mentor who is genuinely invested in your development. A great mentor will dedicate time and energy to helping you succeed.

5. **Willingness to Challenge You**: A good mentor doesn't just guide; they challenge. They push you out of your comfort zone and encourage you to aim higher, helping you see your potential and strive for excellence.

## Embracing the Role of a Mentor

Being a mentor is not just about offering advice it's about responsibility, compassion, and commitment to the growth of others. If you're stepping into a mentoring role, understand that your influence can shape someone's life. It's not just about imparting knowledge; it's about nurturing another's potential and helping them shine in their own right. As you seek a mentor, may you find someone who not only guides but also inspires. May they become a kindred spirit, whose wisdom lights your way and empowers you to reach your brightest future.

# Chapter 6

# Identifying Your Mentee

*"Your title or position does not measure your influence, but by the impact you have on the lives of those you lead."*

Identifying the right mentee is an art that requires discernment, empathy, and a deep understanding of the mentoring relationship. A mentee is more than just someone to teach; they are a partner in growth, a reflection of your influence, and a testament to the power of mentorship. Finding the right individual to guide means looking beyond surface potential to uncover the qualities that make mentorship impactful. A successful mentee demonstrates eagerness to learn. Look for individuals who show a hunger for growth. This could be seen in their curiosity, willingness to ask questions, and drive to seek knowledge independently. Challenges and setbacks are inevitable, but the right mentee will face these moments with determination and grit.

They must possess an intrinsic motivation to overcome obstacles and pursue their goals despite adversity. A mentee should be willing to accept constructive feedback and take it as an opportunity for improvement rather than criticism. This openness fosters a two-way dynamic of trust and respect. Mentorship is a partnership that requires time and energy. A mentee should be willing to engage fully, investing the necessary effort to grow within the mentorship relationship.

In my experience, the journey of identifying and nurturing mentees has been both challenging and rewarding. Take Sharon, for instance. I found her in a vulnerable state, battling emotional and mental turmoil. She had shared her struggles in an online group, and something in her plea for help moved me. Reaching out to her marked the beginning of a mentorship relationship that would change both our lives. Sharon's journey from despair to faith has been remarkable. Over five years, she has transformed into a beacon of hope a testament to her resilience and God's grace. Her openness and commitment made her the perfect mentee, someone willing to be guided while taking charge of her own growth.

Then there was Emily, a young professional with big dreams but little confidence.

She approached me at a networking event, seeking direction but unsure of her capabilities. Through our mentorship, I saw her evolve from hesitant and self-doubting to assured and ambitious. Her willingness to embrace feedback and step out of her comfort zone revealed the potential she had all along.

Not every potential mentee will align with your capacity to guide or your style of mentorship. It's vital to balance your willingness to help with an honest evaluation of the mentee's readiness and compatibility. As mentors, we must ask: Does this person have the perseverance to make the most of this relationship? Are they seeking mentorship for the right reasons, or do they lack the commitment needed? Will this relationship encourage mutual growth? Recognizing the mentee who aligns with your values, goals, and ability to guide is essential for fostering a successful partnership. At its core, the mentor-mentee relationship is not a one-sided transfer of knowledge but a reciprocal journey of growth. A great mentee inspires their mentor, offering fresh perspectives and reigniting their passion for guiding others.

Mentorship is about impact, connection, and shared growth. As you seek your mentee, remember that the right individual will not only benefit from your guidance but also enrich your life in return. *"As you seek to identify your mentee, may you find not just a student, but a fellow traveler whose growth enriches your own journey as well."*

# PART II

# EXPLORING MENTORSHIP DYNAMICS

# Chapter 7

# Types of Mentors

*"The greatest good you can do for another is not just share your riches, but to reveal to them their own."* -Benjamin Disraeli

Mentors come in all shapes and sizes, each bringing their own unique blend of wisdom, experience, and perspective to the table. From the seasoned professional to the nurturing caregiver, mentors play a crucial role in guiding, inspiring, and empowering those they mentor. Understanding the different types of mentors helps mentees identify the right fit for their needs and aspirations, ensuring a fruitful and fulfilling mentorship journey. Some mentors excel in providing practical guidance and support, while others specialize in offering emotional comfort and encouragement. Some mentors are known for their visionary leadership, while others shine in their ability to listen, empathize, and offer sage advice.

Whatever their style or approach, the best mentors share a common commitment to nurturing the growth and development of those they mentor, serving as beacons of light and inspiration along the journey of life. Having a mentor is one thing; sitting under mentorship is another. Many claim to have mentors, but it often ends in their minds and words, not in action. They lack the time or closeness to learn, seek guidance, and address issues with their mentors. They do not fully submit to or avail themselves of their mentors for impartation, correction, or rebuke.

I was one of them. Trust me, this gave room to many setbacks and instability in my life, no matter how much I loved God. Anointing without structure is like a body without bones; it is the bones that bring figure and structure, not the flesh. Though I am grateful to have found a true mentor, I could see when the Lord brought her into my presence. Have you ever felt so confused, like the world is crumbling down on you? Like your prayers keep bouncing back off the ceiling? Have you ever felt you carry something huge within you but fail to interpret your roadmap to your destiny? I needed someone who would not abandon me when I failed. I had so many unanswered questions.

All the mentors I looked up to seemed to be fainting and drifting away. I couldn't stand watching some contradict the word of God without being able to speak out because of fear of confronting my leaders. I couldn't stand being a good flock because of seeds and offerings. I couldn't breathe in the atmosphere that called for material demands while my life was stagnant. I was tired of prophecies that ended in their audience but did not come to pass.

I had to ask God if I was to continue keeping silent while my spirit was slowly being tortured and dying from the deceit of wolves in sheep's clothing. I was no longer the same innocent, Holy Spirit-filled girl. I was battling with my understanding of what a mentor was and whether they were needed or just a show-off for Christians to be seen as humble and full of integrity. Mentors come in many forms, each bringing unique strengths and perspectives to the relationship. Recognizing the different types of mentors helps in identifying the right fit for your needs and maximizing the impact of the mentorship.

The coach is a mentor who focuses on performance and skill development. They provide structured guidance, set goals, and offer feedback to help the mentee improve specific competencies. Coaches are often found in professional settings, where they help mentees enhance their job performance, develop new skills, and achieve career advancement. They are results-oriented and provide actionable advice to help mentees reach their full potential.

The connector is another type of mentor who leverages their extensive network to create opportunities for the mentee. They introduce the mentee to influential contacts, helping them build valuable relationships and expand their professional horizons. Connectors are particularly valuable in industries where networking is crucial for career success. They help mentees navigate social and professional networks, opening doors to new opportunities and experiences.

The cheerleader is a mentor who provides emotional support and encouragement. They help the mentee build confidence and maintain motivation, especially during challenging times. Cheerleaders are empathetic and nurturing, offering positive reinforcement and celebrating the mentee's successes.

They play a crucial role in boosting the mentee's morale and helping them stay focused and motivated on their journey. The challenger, on the other hand, pushes the mentee to exceed their limits and grow beyond their comfort zone. They encourage critical thinking, question assumptions, and promote continuous learning. Challengers help mentees develop resilience and adaptability, preparing them to face complex and unpredictable situations. They provide tough love and constructive criticism, driving the mentee to achieve excellence and realize their full potential.

Understanding the type of mentor you need can greatly enhance the effectiveness of the mentorship relationship. Whether you require skill development, networking opportunities, emotional support, or a push towards growth, identifying the right type of mentor ensures that your specific needs are met. From the hallowed halls of academia to the bustling corridors of industry, the mentor's influence knows no bounds. They are the architects of innovation, the guardians of tradition, and the stewards of progress.

Through their guidance and mentorship, they impart not only knowledge but also wisdom the wisdom to navigate uncertainty, to embrace change, and to forge one's path with courage and conviction. Life is worth living alongside someone who believes in you. Visions, dreams, and goals are worth pursuing when you have a mentor pushing you to become better, not bitter. Mentors, life coaches, trainers, and leaders exist to make the world a better place, but not everyone is ready for them. They may be invisible, but their work manifests behind the scenes through their mentees, followers, or disciples.

## Defining the Mentor

The term "mentor" finds its origins in ancient Greek mythology, particularly in Homer's epic poem, "The Odyssey." Mentor was the name of a character who was entrusted with the care and education of Odysseus's son, Telemachus, during Odysseus's prolonged absence. Mentor served as a teacher, protector, and advisor to Telemachus, embodying the qualities that define mentorship today.

The use of the word "mentor" to describe a trusted advisor or guide can be traced back to this historical context, and it has evolved over time to become a universal term for someone who provides wisdom and support to another. But who, precisely, is a mentor? At its core, a mentor is more than a mere teacher or advisor they are a trusted confidant, a source of inspiration, and a catalyst for transformation. A mentor embodies wisdom, empathy, and resilience, guiding their mentees through the labyrinth of life with unwavering support and unwavering devotion. They are not just leaders; they are architects of dreams, helping to sculpt futures and unlock potentials that lie dormant within.

PATIENCE SAKUTUKWA

## Poem: The Mentor's Light (The Odyssey)

*In halls of old where wisdom blooms, a guiding light through all our glooms, with patience, care, and knowledge deep, our dreams and fears, in trust, we keep.*
*From ancient tales and myths they rise, a mentor's soul with piercing eyes, they see our strengths, our hidden fears, and guide us through the fleeting years.*
*With words of hope and actions kind, they shape our hearts and free our minds, in every triumph, every fall, a mentor's hand is there through all.*
*In shadows cast by doubt and dread, their wisdom lights the path ahead, they teach us not to mimic, blind, but find our truths, our voice, and our kind.*
*Their legacy in us endures, through lessons learned and hopes assured, for in each mentor's heart we find, the strength to soar, the will to bind.*
*So here's to mentors, far and near, whose guidance we hold ever dear, in every step, their light we see, they are the bridge to what can be.*

## Traditional Definition

A mentor is an experienced and trusted advisor who provides guidance, support, and knowledge to a less experienced person, known as a mentee. The mentor's role is to foster the personal and professional growth of the mentee by sharing their expertise, offering constructive feedback, and encouraging the mentee to achieve their goals.

## Modern Perspective

In contemporary terms, a mentor is seen as a facilitator of learning and development. They are not just sources of wisdom but partners in the mentee's journey, helping to navigate both career paths and personal growth with a focus on holistic development.

## Psychological Insight

From a psychological standpoint, a mentor acts as a mirror, reflecting the mentee's strengths and areas for improvement.

They provide a safe space for the mentee to explore their potential and confront their limitations, fostering self-awareness and confidence.

## Educational Context

In an educational setting, a mentor is an educator who goes beyond traditional teaching to nurture a student's intellectual and personal growth. They guide students through academic challenges and inspire a love for lifelong learning.

## Corporate View

Within the corporate world, a mentor is a leader who imparts knowledge about industry practices, helps navigate organizational structures, and provides career advice to facilitate professional advancement.

## Characteristics of a Mentor

Effective mentors possess a variety of key characteristics that enable them to positively influence their mentees. They act as guides who provide direction and help the mentee navigate their personal and professional journey.

As advisors, mentors offer expert advice based on their knowledge and experience. They serve as role models, demonstrating behaviors and practices that mentees can emulate.

Mentors also act as supporters, encouraging and motivating their mentees, while actively listening to their concerns, ideas, and challenges. They challenge their mentees to step out of their comfort zones and reach their potential, provide valuable resources and opportunities, offer constructive feedback for growth and improvement, and help mentees stay focused and accountable to their goals. The world would be a better place if everyone had a mentor, but not everyone has a vision or dream.

## What Sets a Mentor Apart?

What sets a mentor apart from the ordinary? It is their ability to inspire, to empathize, and to lead by example. A mentor possesses a wealth of experience tempered by humility, a keen insight into the human condition, and an unshakeable belief in the potential of others.

They are listeners, storytellers, and truth-seekers, weaving narratives of resilience and triumph that resonate across generations.

## Wisdom from Mentors

Mentors have shared wisdom that highlights the value of their role. For instance, Oprah Winfrey once said, "A mentor is someone who allows you to see the hope inside yourself." This quote underscores the empowering nature of mentorship, where mentors help mentees recognize their potential. Another insightful quote is, "The delicate balance of mentoring someone is not creating them in your own image, but giving them the opportunity to create themselves," which reflects the supportive and enabling role of a mentor. These quotes encapsulate the essence of mentorship, emphasizing its importance in personal and professional growth.

## Reflections on the Journey

In my journey as a mentor, I've experienced moments of profound success and gratification, as well as moments of frustration and disappointment.

Some of my greatest successes as a mentor include witnessing the growth and development of my mentees as they overcome obstacles, achieve their goals, and fulfill their potential.

As I reflect on my own journey as a mentor, I am reminded of the countless lives I have touched and the profound impact they have had on me in return. Each mentee is a testament to the power of mentorship a living embodiment of hope, resilience, and human potential. And though my path may have been fraught with challenges and obstacles, it is the bonds forged with my mentees that have sustained me through the darkest of times. I have also witnessed growth personally. I have learned that being a mentor does not only mean you lead and guide but it also means you learn as you mentor them. In a world of pursuits, we can do it fast and excellent alongside a mentor. The Mentor is the center core of our next steps and our key to our destiny.

## THE MENTOR & THE MENTEE

Mentors are vital and they define mentees as well as determine the quality of your future. Mentors are the clue to the hidden part within us that is yet to be unleashed.

Perhaps you have been desiring a mentor, perhaps you have been trying to understand this mystery of mentorship, and the following chapters will unveil the mystery of mentorship.

A mentor is more than a guide; they are a cornerstone in the edifice of personal and professional growth. In today's fast-paced world, the role of a mentor has never been more critical. A mentor provides a blend of support, advice, and inspiration, helping mentees navigate the complexities of their careers and personal lives.

This relationship is deeply transformative, fostering an environment where learning and growth flourish. As Plutarch once said, "The mind is not a vessel to be filled, but a fire to be kindled." A mentor does precisely that kindles the fire of curiosity, ambition, and passion within their mentee. The mentor-mentee relationship is built on mutual respect and trust. It requires the mentor to listen actively, provide constructive feedback, and inspire confidence. It is a partnership where both parties grow and learn from each other.

The mentor gains satisfaction from seeing their mentee succeed, while the mentee benefits from the mentor's experience and wisdom. This symbiotic relationship is the bedrock of effective mentorship. The archetype of the mentor has graced tales and sagas since antiquity, shaping the journeys of heroes and heroines alike. From the wise counsel of Merlin to the steadfast guidance of Obi-Wan Kenobi, mentors have stood as beacons of wisdom and support, guiding their charges through the trials and tribulations of life's odyssey. The mentor embodies a wealth of experience, knowledge, and insight, garnered through years of trials, triumphs, and tribulations. They possess a keen understanding of the human condition, coupled with a genuine desire to uplift and empower those who seek their guidance. Whether found in the hallowed halls of academia, the bustling corridors of corporate boardrooms, or the serene sanctuaries of spiritual retreats, mentors serve as catalysts for growth, enlightenment, and transformation.

To be a mentor is to embark on a sacred journey of selflessness and service, offering a hand to those who tread the path behind.

It is a calling that transcends titles and accolades, rooted in a deep-seated commitment to the betterment of humanity. As mentors, we do not seek to mold others in our likeness but to nurture their innate talents, strengths, and potentialities, empowering them to chart their own course and fulfill their unique destinies. In the mentor, we find a steadfast ally, a compassionate listener, and a wise guide who walks beside us, illuminating the shadows and pointing the way forward.

They offer not just knowledge and expertise but also empathy, encouragement, and unwavering support. In their presence, we find inspiration, validation, and the courage to embrace our true selves. The mentor's legacy is not measured in accolades or achievements but in the lives they touch, the hearts they uplift, and the souls they inspire. They leave behind a lasting imprint on the fabric of existence, weaving a tapestry of wisdom, compassion, and hope for generations to come. As we journey through the labyrinth of life, may we be blessed with mentors who light our path, guide our steps, and remind us of the boundless potential that resides within us.

# Chapter 8

# Types of Mentees

*"One book, one pen, one child, and one teacher can change the world." -*
*Malala Yousafzai*

Just as mentors come in all shapes and sizes, mentees also bring a unique blend of aspirations, challenges, and potential to their relationships. The dynamics of mentorship are deeply enriched by understanding the individuality of each mentee, allowing mentors to adapt their approach and create a supportive, empowering experience. Mentees are diverse, each shaped by their personal goals, learning styles, and the context of their growth journey. Some are eager learners, driven by an insatiable thirst for knowledge. They thrive on absorbing wisdom, actively seeking opportunities to apply insights to their personal and professional development. Others are more reflective, valuing the time to process lessons thoughtfully.

These mentees find solace in deep conversations and introspection, deriving meaning from the subtleties of their mentorship experience. There are those who embrace challenges, finding strength in adversity, while others require gentler guidance to build their confidence and navigate uncertainty. Some mentees demonstrate an exploratory nature, venturing into uncharted territories with curiosity and a willingness to take risks. These mentees often require mentors who can guide them through unfamiliar landscapes, helping them expand their horizons while staying grounded. On the other hand, some mentees question assumptions, embracing skepticism as a means of driving deeper understanding. These individuals benefit from mentors who engage in stimulating discussions, offering well-reasoned perspectives that encourage critical thinking.

Recognizing the diverse nature of mentees fosters a more harmonious and effective mentorship relationship. Each mentee's distinct characteristics demand an approach tailored to their needs, ensuring that the partnership is both productive and fulfilling.

## THE MENTOR & THE MENTEE

The experience of being a mentee is multifaceted, deeply rooted in the pursuit of growth and transformation. Historically, mentorship has taken many forms, from the guidance provided by ancient Greek mentors like Telemachus in *The Odyssey* to the master-apprentice relationships of medieval guilds. Through these various contexts, mentees have played an integral role, actively engaging in the learning process to achieve their personal and professional aspirations.

The modern term "mentee" reflects the evolving understanding of this role. Derived from the word "mentor," its etymology points to a dynamic relationship defined by trust, growth, and collaboration. A mentee is much more than a recipient of knowledge; they are active participants in their development, fueled by a desire to learn and an openness to change. Their journey is marked by humility, curiosity, and resilience. The willingness to step outside their comfort zones and embrace new perspectives distinguishes them as learners dedicated to self-improvement.

The relationship between a mentor and mentee is transformative, offering both parties the opportunity for growth. Mentees often experience accelerated personal and professional advancement due to the insights and support provided by their mentors. Research shows that individuals who engage in mentorship are more likely to achieve career success, higher salaries, and greater job satisfaction. Beyond professional benefits, mentees gain confidence, build networks, and develop skills that shape their personal lives.

Being a mentee requires an active and engaged role. It is a journey that begins with acknowledging the need for guidance and taking the first step toward seeking a mentor. Lao Tzu's adage, "A journey of a thousand miles begins with a single step," aptly captures the essence of this path. A mentee's willingness to ask questions, apply knowledge, and embrace feedback defines the success of the relationship. This proactive approach, combined with perseverance, allows them to navigate challenges and achieve their goals with clarity and determination.

The role of the mentee is not one of dependence but of empowerment. By respecting their mentor's time and wisdom, mentees foster relationships built on mutual trust and respect. They embrace the mentorship journey with gratitude and an eagerness to grow, leaving an indelible mark on their fields and communities. As mentees continue to shape their destinies, they carry forward the legacy of mentorship, inspiring future generations with the transformative power of guidance, learning, and collaboration.

# Chapter 9

# Types of Mentorship

*"In learning you will teach, and in teaching you will learn."* - Phil Collins

Mentorship, like a multifaceted gem, refracts into countless forms, each uniquely brilliant and profoundly transformative. It serves as a beacon, illuminating pathways of personal and professional growth while shaping destinies and nurturing talents. Across cultures, generations, and disciplines, mentorship takes on various hues, tailored to address specific needs, goals, and aspirations. It is through understanding and embracing these diverse types of mentorship that individuals can unlock their potential and find guidance suited to their unique journeys. At the heart of mentorship lies the power of one-on-one relationships. Traditional mentorship is perhaps the most widely recognized, offering a deeply personal and individualized approach.

This bond between mentor and mentee fosters a trusting, supportive environment, where the wisdom and experience of one enrich the life of the other. Often taking place within formal programs or organically in personal or professional settings, this relationship has guided countless individuals to overcome challenges, acquire skills, and achieve personal growth. In an era of rapid technological advancement and shifting paradigms, reverse mentorship introduces an innovative approach. This form defies convention, recognizing the value of intergenerational exchange, where younger or less experienced individuals share their expertise with seasoned professionals. Whether in areas of technology, social media, or emerging trends, reverse mentorship bridges generational divides and fosters a culture of mutual respect and learning.

The power of community and collective wisdom comes alive in group mentorship. Here, multiple mentees gather under the guidance of one or more mentors, fostering a collaborative environment. This shared journey allows for the exchange of diverse perspectives, peer learning, and collective brainstorming, making it particularly effective in settings where teamwork and mutual support are crucial.

Amidst the digital revolution, virtual mentorship emerges as a versatile and inclusive form, transcending geographical barriers. Leveraging technology, this approach brings mentors and mentees together in virtual spaces, offering unparalleled flexibility and accessibility. Whether through video calls, online forums, or mentorship platforms, this method has revolutionized how individuals connect, share knowledge, and grow, irrespective of their physical location.

Career mentorship shines as a guiding light in the labyrinth of professional aspirations. Tailored to address specific career-related goals, this type of mentorship provides mentees with insights into industries, strategies for advancement, and advice on navigating transitions. Whether climbing the corporate ladder, developing leadership skills, or exploring new career paths, this relationship equips individuals with the tools and confidence to thrive in their chosen fields. Beyond professional ambitions, life mentorship embraces the holistic journey of personal fulfillment and well-being. In this type of relationship, mentors offer guidance across a wide range of life's challenges, from emotional resilience to financial planning.

These mentors often serve as a steady compass, helping mentees find balance and purpose while navigating the complexities of life. Structured mentorship programs within organizations and institutions provide a formal framework for cultivating these relationships. From onboarding initiatives to leadership development, these programs pair mentors and mentees in relationships guided by clear goals and expectations. Such programs help instill a culture of learning, growth, and support within professional environments. Conversely, mentorship relationships also blossom organically in the unstructured flow of daily interactions. Informal mentorship is born out of authentic connections, driven by mutual respect and shared values. These relationships often arise serendipitously, thriving on the genuineness of mutual rapport rather than predefined structures.

The beauty of mentorship extends further into cross-cultural exchanges, where individuals from diverse backgrounds come together to share experiences and insights. Cross-cultural mentorship fosters empathy, understanding, and inclusivity, breaking down barriers and celebrating differences.

This type of mentorship serves as a bridge, connecting individuals and promoting global citizenship in an increasingly interconnected world. As we explore the vast labyrinth of mentorship, each pathway reveals a new perspective, enriching the mentor-mentee relationship and fostering growth on both sides. Whether deeply personal or broadly communal, rooted in tradition or inspired by innovation, mentorship remains an enduring force, sculpting lives, guiding aspirations, and leaving a legacy of transformation.

# PART III

# SPECIALIZED MENTORSHIP

# Chapter 10

# Traditional Mentorship

*"It's essential to develop a support system of mentors and peers who can offer guidance, encouragement, and accountability."*

Traditional mentorship stands as one of humanity's oldest and most profound practices, a timeless bridge connecting generations through the transfer of wisdom, knowledge, and skills. It is deeply embedded in the cultural fabric of societies across the globe, serving as a lifeline for the preservation of values, traditions, and collective identity. This form of mentorship, often rooted in oral traditions, apprenticeship, and lived experience, represents a dynamic interplay between the past, present, and future. The origins of traditional mentorship can be traced back to ancient societies where elders played a pivotal role in guiding their communities.

Among the Indigenous peoples of Africa, elders were revered as custodians of wisdom, their mentorship shaping the next generation of leaders, warriors, and community builders. Storytelling, a hallmark of African tradition, was a primary vehicle for passing down cultural knowledge. Tales such as Anansi the Spider in West Africa or the epic of Mwindo from the Congo served not only to entertain but also to teach moral lessons, resilience, and problem-solving. Similarly, in ancient Greece, mentorship was institutionalized through the educational philosophies of great thinkers like Socrates, Plato, and Aristotle. Socrates, a mentor to Plato, famously employed the Socratic method, a form of questioning that encouraged critical thinking and self-discovery. Plato, in turn, mentored Aristotle, whose teachings laid the foundation for modern philosophy and science. This lineage of mentorship illustrates the cascading effect of traditional guidance, where the insights of one generation elevate the next. In the medieval era, the apprenticeship system flourished as a cornerstone of traditional mentorship.

## THE MENTOR & THE MENTEE

Artisans, blacksmiths, and masons would take on apprentices, teaching them the intricacies of their craft through hands-on experience. These relationships were deeply personal, often resembling familial bonds. Michelangelo, the Renaissance master, honed his skills under the mentorship of Domenico Ghirlandaio, a renowned painter and sculptor of the time. The legacy of their relationship endures in the timeless beauty of Michelangelo's works, such as the Sistine Chapel ceiling.

Traditional mentorship extends beyond individual achievements to encompass broader cultural and spiritual dimensions. In Native American societies, mentorship often took the form of vision quests and ceremonial guidance provided by elders or shamans. These mentors helped young members of the tribe connect with their spiritual essence, understand their role in the community, and align their lives with the rhythms of nature. Throughout history, traditional mentorship has also played a vital role in leadership development. In East Asia, the Confucian model of mentorship emphasized filial piety, moral character, and the cultivation of virtue.

Confucius himself was a mentor to many, imparting principles that continue to influence educational and leadership practices today. His teachings underscore the transformative power of mentorship rooted in ethical conduct and lifelong learning. Modern thinkers and authors have reflected on the enduring value of traditional mentorship. Stephen Covey, in *The 7 Habits of Highly Effective People*, highlights the importance of interpersonal relationships and the mentor's role in nurturing potential. Similarly, John C. Maxwell, a leadership expert, asserts that "mentorship is the bridge that connects a person's current reality to their future possibilities." These perspectives echo the essence of traditional mentorship as a relationship grounded in trust, respect, and shared growth.

Despite its ancient roots, traditional mentorship remains highly relevant in today's world. The dynamics may have evolved with advancements in technology and shifts in societal structures, but the essence of mentorship, guiding, nurturing, and inspiring, remains unchanged. In families, workplaces, and communities, traditional mentors continue to provide a moral compass, equipping individuals with the resilience to face life's complexities.

As we reflect on the legacy of traditional mentorship, it is evident that its impact transcends time. It is a living thread woven into the human experience, a beacon that illuminates the path of progress while anchoring us to our cultural and spiritual roots. From the wisdom of elders to the structured apprenticeship of masters and their protégés, traditional mentorship embodies the enduring power of human connection and the transformative potential of shared knowledge.

# Chapter 11

# Spiritual Mentorship

*"The spiritual journey is individual, highly personal. It can't be organized or regulated. It isn't true that everyone should follow one path. Listen to your own truth."* - Ram Dass

Spiritual mentorship is a profound journey of self-discovery, a transformative relationship where a mentor serves as a guide, illuminating the mentee's path toward spiritual growth and enlightenment. Rooted in ancient traditions, spiritual mentorship transcends the boundaries of the material world, delving into the essence of the soul. It is a deeply personal experience where the mentor and mentee form a bond that fosters growth, understanding, and a deeper connection to the divine. The mentor, an experienced spiritual guide, nurtures the mentee by providing support, wisdom, and encouragement.

Together, they explore spiritual practices and rituals, seek clarity on life's greatest mysteries, and develop a sense of purpose that extends beyond the mundane. This relationship is built on trust and respect, forming a foundation that allows the mentee to navigate life's challenges with grace and resilience.

## Origins of Spiritual Mentorship

The roots of spiritual mentorship stretch far back into history, weaving through various religious and cultural traditions. In Christianity, spiritual mentorship flourished in the early church. Jesus, as a mentor, guided His twelve disciples, teaching them through parables and preparing them for their divine mission. Similarly, the Apostle Paul mentored Timothy, offering him spiritual guidance and instruction to lead the early church. These biblical relationships emphasize the power of experiential learning and the transformational nature of mentorship in faith development. Beyond Christianity, spiritual mentorship is also reflected in other traditions.

## THE MENTOR & THE MENTEE

In Eastern philosophies, sages and gurus often served as mentors, guiding seekers through meditation, introspection, and contemplation. Sufi mystics, for instance, acted as spiritual guides, leading their followers toward union with the divine. These practices underscore the universal need for mentorship in navigating the labyrinth of existence.

## Types of Spiritual Mentorship

Spiritual mentorship takes on many forms, each tailored to meet the unique needs of the mentee. In discipleship mentorship, the focus lies on imparting religious teachings and helping the mentee live according to spiritual principles. Counseling mentorship, on the other hand, provides guidance during life's challenges, enabling the mentee to discern God's will in difficult situations. Accountability mentorship fosters faithfulness by encouraging the mentee to stay true to their spiritual commitments, offering support to overcome temptations.

Leadership mentorship prepares individuals for roles in ministry or church leadership, equipping them with the skills and wisdom to lead others spiritually. Peer mentorship creates a mutual relationship where individuals of similar spiritual maturity encourage and inspire each other's growth.

## The Christian Perspective

Within Christianity, spiritual mentorship holds a distinct and revered place. Mentors often lead mentees through scripture study, engaging in thoughtful discussions to apply biblical teachings in everyday life. Prayer becomes a shared practice, fostering a deep and consistent connection with God. Acts of service emerge as a vital component, helping mentees live out their faith by serving others and strengthening their spiritual journey. The sense of community is another crucial element, as mentorship encourages participation in communal worship and church activities. This shared journey of faith creates a bond that nurtures spiritual growth and a sense of belonging within the larger church family.

## What Happens in Spiritual Mentorship

## PATIENCE SAKUTUKWA

In the sacred space of spiritual mentorship, mentors act as compassionate guides, imparting wisdom and insight tailored to the mentee's unique path. Through meditation, prayer, and reflection, mentees delve into the depths of their being, confronting fears, embracing inner peace, and nurturing qualities such as compassion and forgiveness. This relationship offers more than guidance; it cultivates a profound connection to the divine, fostering moments of clarity and insight. Spiritual mentorship is not simply about acquiring knowledge but about awakening the soul to its infinite possibilities. Mentees learn to trust their intuition, honor their inner wisdom, and walk life's path with courage and grace.

## Importance of Spiritual Mentorship

The importance of spiritual mentorship lies in its ability to inspire and empower individuals on their journey toward enlightenment. It provides a safe space for exploration, where mentees grapple with existential questions and deepen their understanding of spiritual truths. This mentorship also fosters a sense of community, bringing together like-minded seekers who share in the transformative journey of spiritual awakening. Moreover, spiritual mentorship integrates spiritual insights into daily life, leading to greater authenticity and fulfillment. The mentor's guidance often brings peace and clarity, enabling the mentee to overcome life's uncertainties and navigate challenges with resilience.

## Personal Experiences in Spiritual Mentorship

For many, spiritual mentorship is a life-changing experience. Under the guidance of their mentors, mentees often recount moments of divine grace, spiritual awakening, and profound healing. These encounters can lead to liberation from inner struggles and a deeper connection to their true nature as spiritual beings. In some instances, the journey involves confronting and transcending the ego, experiencing a rebirth that reveals the soul's essence. Spiritual mentorship becomes a beacon of light, guiding individuals toward self-realization and harmony with the universe.

Spiritual mentorship, in its essence, is about more than guidance. It is an invitation to embark on a journey of transformation, where the mentor and mentee co-create a path of spiritual growth. Together, they explore the infinite possibilities within, discovering a sense of peace and fulfillment that transcends the material realm.

# Chapter 12

# Physical Mentorship

*"Take care of your body. It's the only place you have to live."* - Jim Rohn

In the bustling city of New York, amidst the towering skyscrapers and lively streets, lies a hidden gem, a small gym tucked away in a quiet corner. Within its walls, amidst the clanging of weights and the rhythmic hum of treadmills, a unique bond takes root between a seasoned fitness trainer, Coach Marcus, and his eager mentee, Emily. Coach Marcus, a former athlete with a wealth of experience and a heart of gold, recognizes Emily's burning desire to reclaim control of her physical health. With a gentle yet firm approach, he crafts personalized workout routines tailored to her fitness level and goals. Their journey begins with small, consistent steps such as morning jogs in the park, strength training sessions, and mindful yoga practices.

Through this process, Coach Marcus shares invaluable wisdom gleaned from years of personal training and self-discovery. His words of encouragement instill in Emily a sense of discipline, perseverance, and self-belief. Over weeks and months, her transformation is profound. Her once sluggish stride becomes confident, her muscles grow firm, and her spirit soars with newfound vitality. With each milestone, Coach Marcus celebrates her victories, offering unwavering support. Yet, physical mentorship transcends mere workout routines. It delves deep into the human spirit, unlocking hidden reserves of resilience and determination. Through their shared journey, Emily discovers her inner strength and capacity for growth. She learns to confront challenges head-on, finding empowerment in her achievements.

As she stands atop a metaphorical mountain, Emily gazes at the horizon with newfound clarity and purpose. Her journey with Coach Marcus has been about far more than physical transformation. It has been a journey of self-discovery and growth.

Their bond, forged through determination and effort, illuminates the profound impact of physical mentorship, offering guidance towards health, vitality, and holistic well-being. Through the lens of Emily and Coach Marcus's relationship, we witness the transformative power of physical mentorship. It is a journey that transcends the boundaries of the gym and touches the very core of human experience.

Physical mentorship focuses on the holistic well-being of the individual, encompassing exercise, nutrition, and self-care. Mentors in this realm provide guidance to help mentees cultivate healthy habits, overcome challenges, and achieve optimal vitality. From personalized workout plans to tailored dietary advice, physical mentors offer both practical tools and the motivation needed to succeed. The journey of physical mentorship is one of growth, empowerment, and self-discovery, a journey that inspires individuals to prioritize their health and embrace the full potential of their bodies and spirits.

# Chapter 13

# Professional Mentorship

*"The delicate balance of mentoring someone is not creating them in your own image but giving them the opportunity to create themselves." -* Steven Spielberg

In the bustling corridors of a prestigious law firm, amidst the hum of ringing phones and the rhythmic tapping of keyboards, stands Jacob, a young attorney fueled by dreams of making a difference. Eager to carve his path and leave an indelible mark on the legal profession, Jacob finds himself under the guidance of Lisa, a mentor whose professional excellence and unwavering integrity make her an inspiration. Lisa, a seasoned attorney with decades of experience, embodies the principles of ethical leadership and dedication. Taking Jacob under her wing, she imparts invaluable wisdom drawn from her years of navigating the complexities of the legal field.

Together, they tackle intricate legal cases, unravel the intricacies of office dynamics, and strategize for long-term success. Yet, professional mentorship is about more than career advancement. It is a journey of character-building and leadership development. Lisa's mentorship goes beyond teaching legal concepts; it emphasizes the importance of humility, empathy, and using one's skills to create a positive impact.

As Jacob ascends through the ranks of the firm, he carries with him the lessons Lisa has instilled. Every success becomes an opportunity for him to give back, mentoring young attorneys and continuing the cycle of guidance and growth. Their relationship stands as a testament to the transformative power of professional mentorship. It highlights a journey of shared learning, leadership, and empowerment that transcends the confines of the office walls. Professional mentorship is a structured, goal-oriented relationship that fosters career development and personal growth. It connects experienced professionals with mentees, offering those insights, advice, and strategies to navigate their career paths.

## PATIENCE SAKUTUKWA

Mentors serve as guides, helping mentees identify goals, build skills, and overcome challenges with confidence. Key aspects of professional mentorship include career guidance, industry knowledge sharing, and performance feedback. Mentors assist mentees in crafting actionable plans, setting realistic goals, and developing strategies for success. They also create networking opportunities, introducing mentees to influential contacts and opening doors to new prospects. A successful mentorship relationship thrives on consistent communication, clear objectives, and mutual commitment. Mentors provide constructive feedback and unwavering support, motivating mentees to stay focused on their aspirations.

The rewards of professional mentorship are transformative. Mentees gain critical industry insights, develop essential skills, and grow in confidence. They also benefit from an expanded professional network, leading to new opportunities and resources. This guidance can accelerate career advancement, enhance job satisfaction, and cultivate a lifelong passion for learning and growth.

Professional mentorship ultimately empowers individuals to thrive in their careers, navigate challenges with resilience, and seize opportunities with conviction. It is a collaborative journey where both mentor and mentee grow, creating a ripple effect of learning and leadership that influences generations.

# Chapter 14

# Creative Mentorship

*"Creativity is contagious, pass it on."* - Albert Einstein

Creative mentorship is a vibrant and inspirational relationship that ignites the spark of artistic vision and nurtures the expression of talent. It is a collaboration where mentors guide, encourage, and provide constructive feedback to help mentees unlock their creative potential, refine their craft, and pursue their artistic dreams. Whether through brainstorming sessions, technique exploration, or portfolio reviews, creative mentors create a supportive environment where ideas flourish, boundaries are pushed, and innovation thrives. In the heart of an artist's enclave, where colors dance and imaginations take flight, resides Mia, a promising painter yearning to share her vision with the world. Yet, despite her raw talent and burning passion, she finds herself ensnared by the grip of self-doubt and creative block. Enter Jackson, a seasoned artist whose studio pulses with creativity and whose guidance promises transformation.

Recognizing Mia's struggle, Jackson extends his mentorship, welcoming her into his studio and offering her a haven to rediscover her artistic voice. Together, they delve into the depths of her imagination, unearthing hidden talents with each stroke of her brush. Jackson encourages Mia to experiment boldly, relinquish the need for perfection, and embrace the unpredictable nature of the creative process.

Under his mentorship, Mia begins to silence the inner critic that once held her captive. As the days turn into weeks and the weeks into months, her artistic expression flourishes. She paints with uninhibited freedom, pouring her soul into every canvas. Her work transforms from cautious and constrained to daring and evocative, reflecting her journey of self-discovery and liberation.

Their bond is a living testament to the transformative power of creative mentorship. It is a journey not confined to the canvas but

## THE MENTOR & THE MENTEE

extending to the very core of self-expression and identity. Jackson's influence helps Mia realize that creativity is not merely a skill but a way of viewing and interacting with the world, inspiring her to share her vision unapologetically.

# The Essence of Creative Mentorship

Creative mentorship transcends technical guidance. It is about fostering self-expression, cultivating originality, and empowering mentees to embrace their unique voices. Mentors inspire mentees to take risks, challenge norms, and explore the uncharted territories of their creativity. This process requires trust, mutual respect, and the freedom to fail, as failure often leads to profound breakthroughs. Mentors provide insight into navigating the creative industries, offering practical advice on building portfolios, networking, and promoting artistic work. They also encourage a deeper connection to the creative process, helping mentees infuse their work with authenticity and purpose.

# The Impact

The benefits of creative mentorship extend beyond the mentee's immediate growth. By nurturing creativity, mentors help mentees build confidence, resilience, and an innovative mindset. Mentees gain the courage to experiment, the discipline to refine their skills, and the vision to contribute meaningfully to their artistic fields. Through shared inspiration and mutual growth, creative mentorship becomes a powerful force for transformation. It is a journey of artistic exploration that resonates within and beyond the studio, gallery, or stage.

# Chapter 15

# Marital Mentorship

*"A successful marriage requires falling in love many times, always with the same person."* - Mignon McLaughlin

Marital mentorship is a supportive and enriching relationship designed to help couples build and sustain a strong, thriving partnership. This form of mentorship equips couples with the tools to navigate the joys and challenges of marriage while fostering deeper emotional and spiritual connections. Marital mentors, often seasoned couples with years of experience, provide guidance, wisdom, and encouragement, empowering their mentees to nurture a harmonious and fulfilling relationship.

From enhancing communication to developing conflict resolution strategies, marital mentors offer practical advice that strengthens the bond between partners. They help couples develop a shared vision for their lives, grounded in mutual respect, love, and a commitment to grow together.

## The Role of a Marital Mentor

Marital mentors serve as role models, offering insights based on their own experiences. They create a safe and nonjudgmental space for couples to explore their challenges and aspirations. The focus is not on prescribing solutions but on guiding couples to discover what works best for their unique relationship dynamics.

Key areas of focus in marital mentorship include:

- **Effective Communication**: Teaching couples how to listen actively, express themselves openly, and resolve misunderstandings constructively.
- **Conflict Resolution**: Providing strategies to navigate disagreements in a way that fosters growth and understanding rather than division.

- **Intimacy Building**: Encouraging emotional and physical closeness, essential for maintaining a loving connection.
- **Shared Vision**: Helping couples align their goals, values, and aspirations to create a unified path forward.

## The Impact of Marital Mentorship

Marital mentorship profoundly impacts the well-being of couples. Through mentorship, partners often gain clarity about their roles, responsibilities, and expectations within the relationship. This understanding fosters trust, mutual respect, and resilience. Couples who engage in mentorship report higher levels of satisfaction in their relationships, as they feel equipped to handle challenges and celebrate milestones together. Mentors inspire mentees to approach their marriage with intentionality, recognizing that a thriving relationship requires effort, patience, and continuous learning. As couples grow under the guidance of marital mentors, they often pass on the lessons they have learned, becoming mentors themselves. This creates a ripple effect, spreading the principles of strong and enduring relationships within their communities.

## The Broader Ripple Effect

While the immediate benefits of marital mentorship are evident in the growth of individual couples, its influence extends much further. Healthy, stable marriages contribute to the well-being of families and communities. Mentorship fosters a culture where love, understanding, and commitment are celebrated, creating a legacy of strong relationships for future generations.

## Reflections on Growth

Marital mentorship, much like any mentorship, thrives on shared experiences and mutual respect. It teaches couples the value of vulnerability, the beauty of compromise, and the power of partnership. By nurturing these qualities, mentorship transforms marriages into partnerships that withstand the trials of life while celebrating its many joys.

This journey is not about creating perfect relationships but about empowering couples to grow together with grace, patience, and unwavering love.

# PART IV

# MENTORSHIP IN VARIOUS CONTEXTS

# Chapter 16

# Community Mentorship

*"Alone, we can do so little; together, we can do so much."* - Helen Keller

Community mentorship is a powerful collective effort that brings individuals together within a shared community to support and uplift each other. Mentors in this realm, coming from various backgrounds and life experiences, provide guidance, encouragement, and resources that enable community members to thrive. Through mentorship programs and grassroots initiatives, these mentors foster an environment of learning, collaboration, and growth that strengthens the fabric of society. Community mentorship not only empowers individuals but also cultivates a sense of belonging, solidarity, and mutual respect, ensuring that each member has the opportunity to achieve their full potential.

In a close-knit community, where neighbors know each other by name and are always ready to lend a helping hand, lies the foundation of a transformative mentorship network. At the heart of this network is Maria, a compassionate leader with a clear vision of fostering connection and belonging. Maria has dedicated herself to creating a platform where community members, regardless of age or background, come together to share their knowledge, skills, and experiences, enriching the lives of everyone involved.

## The Power of Collective Mentorship

Within Maria's community mentorship program, individuals are both mentors and mentees, each contributing their unique gifts while also learning from others. The program spans generations, with older individuals offering career advice, life wisdom, or support in navigating the challenges of adulthood, while younger members contribute fresh perspectives, creativity, and energy to the initiative.

From teaching a young child to read to helping a neighbor with a career transition, the mentorship network ensures that everyone has something valuable to give and something to receive. This mutual exchange of knowledge creates a vibrant, interconnected community where individuals support one another's growth and success. The program becomes more than just a collection of mentorship relationships it transforms into a beacon of hope, resilience, and collective empowerment. Through unity, collaboration, and shared purpose, the community proves that there is no limit to what can be achieved when individuals come together to support one another.

## The Role of Trust in Mentorship

Trust is the cornerstone of all successful mentorship relationships, including community mentorship. Without trust, there can be no open communication, mutual respect, or genuine support. The mentor's responsibility in building trust involves demonstrating consistency, reliability, honesty, and integrity.

A mentor must be someone who follows through on commitments, offers constructive feedback, and provides guidance that truly benefits the mentee's growth. Trust is earned through actions mentors must be dependable and show a consistent commitment to the mentee's development.

For mentees, building trust involves being open, honest, and receptive to feedback. They must be willing to communicate their needs, challenges, and goals clearly and be proactive in accepting and acting upon the advice and guidance of their mentor. Trust in mentorship is a two-way street: it requires both parties to show commitment, openness, and dedication to the relationship.

In community mentorship, where multiple individuals are engaged in supporting one another, trust serves as the foundation for collaboration. Creating a safe and supportive environment where both mentors and mentees feel heard, valued, and respected is essential. This trust fosters a culture of open communication and mutual growth, making it possible for the mentorship network to thrive.

### The Benefits of Trust in Mentorship

When trust is present in a mentorship relationship, the benefits are numerous. Trust promotes open communication, allowing for honest discussions and constructive feedback. It also nurtures mutual respect, which encourages collaboration and a deeper sense of support. A trusting mentorship environment enhances the effectiveness of the relationship, allowing both the mentor and mentee to experience personal and professional growth.

In a community context, this trust extends beyond individual relationships it strengthens the collective spirit of the group. As mentors and mentees grow together, the entire community benefits, cultivating an atmosphere of mutual support, learning, and shared success. Trust becomes the glue that binds the community, creating a thriving ecosystem where everyone can flourish. Through community mentorship, individuals are empowered to achieve their goals, face their challenges, and unlock their potential. As they support each other, they create a network of growth, compassion, and resilience that strengthens both the individual and the community as a whole.

# Chapter 17

# Global Mentorship

*"The world is a book, and those who do not travel read only one page." -*
Saint Augustine

Global mentorship is a dynamic force that transcends geographical boundaries and cultural divides, uniting individuals from around the world in a shared quest for knowledge, growth, and understanding. By leveraging technology, communication tools, and collaboration platforms, global mentors offer guidance, support, and mentorship to individuals across continents and cultures. These mentors help individuals grow both personally and professionally while encouraging an interconnected, global perspective. From online forums to international exchange programs, global mentorship creates opportunities for cross-cultural learning, dialogue, and collaboration that enrich both the lives of mentees and mentors.

Through their work, global mentors foster a sense of global citizenship, empathy, and interconnectedness that builds bridges of understanding, cooperation, and unity.

## The Necessity of Global Mentorship in Today's World

In a world that grows smaller with each passing day, the need for global mentorship has never been greater. As technology advances, the ability to connect with others around the world in real time offers limitless potential for sharing ideas, experiences, and expertise. By breaking down cultural and geographical barriers, global mentorship allows individuals to reach across boundaries and share knowledge in ways that were once unimaginable. Across continents and cultures, individuals come together to exchange insights, experiences, and perspectives, seeking a common goal: to create a better, more equitable world for future generations.

This form of mentorship has proven instrumental in empowering individuals in underdeveloped regions, providing them with the resources, education, and guidance needed to address their challenges and build brighter futures. From entrepreneurs in remote villages in Africa to healthcare workers in Asia's bustling metropolises, global mentorship programs foster cross-cultural partnerships that ignite change in both big and small ways.

As recent academic research suggests, the potential of global mentorship in fostering socio-economic development is vast. For example, a study by Harrell and Jackson (2020) explored how mentorship programs between developed and developing nations can help build business networks, create job opportunities, and improve healthcare outcomes through shared knowledge. By connecting mentors in high-income countries with individuals in developing regions, the programs encourage the exchange of ideas and experiences that promote sustainable development. Moreover, global mentorship fosters a deeper understanding and empathy across cultural divides.

In the words of academic scholar Allison Williams (2019), mentorship is "not merely the transfer of knowledge, but the exchange of worldviews, where both mentor and mentee learn and grow in equal measure." This reciprocal process enriches both parties, allowing them to see beyond their differences and appreciate the common humanity that binds them together.

One of the most prominent examples of global mentorship in action is the role of international non-governmental organizations (NGOs) that operate mentorship programs to address global challenges. Through their partnerships with local organizations, these NGOs connect individuals in areas such as education, healthcare, and business development with experts from around the world. The results of these mentorship programs have been profound.

For instance, the "Global Education Mentorship Initiative" connects teachers in underserved areas with experienced educators in more developed nations. Through video conferences, online resources, and collaborative lesson planning, these teachers share innovative teaching strategies and best practices, significantly improving the quality of education in their classrooms.

According to a report by the World Education Foundation (2021), mentorship programs like these have helped increase literacy rates and improved educational outcomes in some of the most underserved regions of the world. Similarly, mentorship programs focused on business development have had far-reaching effects. By connecting aspiring entrepreneurs in emerging economies with experienced business leaders in developed countries, these initiatives help to build local economies and improve access to critical resources like financing, marketing strategies, and business management skills. According to Smith and Liu (2022), cross-border mentorship in entrepreneurship has not only fueled the growth of businesses but has also fostered economic resilience in developing countries by diversifying income sources and creating sustainable job opportunities.

## The Global Mentorship Revolution

The ripple effects of global mentorship are vast and wide-reaching. They transform lives and communities in ways that can be seen, felt, and experienced on both local and international scales. But global mentorship is not just about the transfer of knowledge and technical skills; it's about fostering a deeper understanding of the diverse cultural landscapes in which we live.

Through global mentorship, individuals from different cultural backgrounds can better understand the social, political, and economic challenges faced by others. This understanding encourages empathy and a commitment to collective global action. As participants in the global mentorship ecosystem, we move beyond merely sharing expertise and instead build lasting relationships of trust, cooperation, and mutual benefit.

Research by international development scholars, including Phelan (2023), emphasizes that mentorship has become a key tool for global cooperation in tackling the most pressing issues of our time, from climate change to global health crises.

As mentorship continues to evolve, its impact will likely increase, with technology continuing to play a crucial role in fostering connection across the globe.

## The Future of Global Mentorship

Looking ahead, global mentorship holds the potential to transform not only the lives of individual mentees but entire communities, industries, and nations. With the continued rise of digital tools and the growing recognition of the need for cross-cultural understanding, global mentorship will be an essential vehicle for tackling global challenges. As global citizens, we must continue to embrace this mentorship model, ensuring that it remains a vital force for positive change. The future of mentorship is not bound by borders; it is a worldwide community committed to mutual growth, learning, and support for all.

# Chapter 18

# Online Mentorship

"Mentoring is a two-way street. The mentor gets wiser while mentoring, and the mentee gains knowledge through the mentor." -Marisol Gonzalez Online mentorship harnesses the power of technology to connect mentors and mentees in virtual spaces, offering guidance, support, and resources to individuals around the globe. Mentors in this realm leverage digital platforms and communication tools to provide personalized mentorship experiences that transcend geographical boundaries and time zones. From video calls to chat forums, online mentors offer flexible and accessible mentorship opportunities that accommodate the diverse needs and schedules of mentees.

Through their mentorship, they empower individuals to pursue their goals, overcome obstacles, and unlock their full potential, regardless of their physical location or circumstances.

As we move into an increasingly interconnected and digital world, the landscape of mentorship continues to evolve. Virtual and online mentorship programs are becoming more prevalent, breaking down geographical barriers and making mentorship accessible to a broader audience. Moreover, the principles of mentorship are being integrated into various aspects of life, from corporate environments to educational institutions and community organizations. The future of mentorship holds the promise of even greater impact as we leverage technology, diversity, and innovative approaches to nurture the next generation of leaders, thinkers, and change-makers.

Mentorship is a journey of shared growth, learning, and transformation. It is a relationship that has the power to change lives, inspire greatness, and build a brighter future. As you embark on your mentorship journey, remember that the true essence of mentorship lies in the genuine connection between mentor and mentee, the mutual respect, and the unwavering commitment to each other's success. Embrace the journey, and let mentorship guide you to new heights of personal and professional fulfillment. Mentorship relationships, like any other relationships, face challenges. These challenges can arise from misunderstandings, misaligned expectations, or external factors. However, overcoming these challenges is crucial for maintaining a successful mentorship relationship and ensuring mutual growth and development. One of the common challenges in mentorship is misaligned expectations. Both the mentor and mentee may have different expectations for the relationship, leading to misunderstandings and frustration. Overcoming this challenge involves clear and open communication. Both parties must communicate their needs, goals, and expectations openly and honestly, ensuring that they are on the same page. Another common challenge is time constraints.

Both the mentor and mentee may have busy schedules, making it difficult to find time for regular check-ins and meetings. Overcoming this challenge involves prioritizing the mentorship relationship and scheduling regular check-ins. Both parties must commit to making time for the relationship, ensuring that it stays on track. External factors, such as organizational changes or personal issues, can also pose challenges to the mentorship relationship. Overcoming these challenges involves being flexible and adaptable.

Both the mentor and mentee must be willing to adjust their plans and goals as needed, ensuring that the relationship remains supportive and productive. Building a successful mentor-mentee relationship also involves addressing any conflicts or issues that arise. Both parties must be willing to discuss and resolve any conflicts openly and honestly, ensuring that the relationship remains positive and productive.

The benefits of overcoming challenges in mentorship are numerous. Overcoming challenges fosters a stronger and more resilient relationship, promoting mutual growth and development. It also builds trust and respect, creating a supportive and collaborative environment for both the mentor and mentee. *"The only limit to our realization of tomorrow will be our doubts of today." - Franklin D. Roosevelt.* Virtual mentorship combines the convenience of online platforms with the intimacy of face-to-face interaction, offering mentees personalized mentorship experiences in virtual environments. Mentors in this realm utilize video conferencing, virtual reality, and other digital tools to create immersive and engaging mentorship experiences that foster connection, collaboration, and growth.

From virtual workshops to interactive seminars, virtual mentors offer mentees opportunities to learn, network, and collaborate in dynamic virtual environments. Through their mentorship, they empower mentees to harness the power of technology to achieve their goals, connect with peers and mentors around the world, and navigate the challenges of the digital age with confidence and resilience.

# Chapter 19

# In-Person Mentorship

*"Mentorship is simply learning from the mistakes and mastery of a successful person in his or her field."* -Bernard Kelvin Clive

In-person mentorship fosters deep connections and meaningful relationships between mentors and mentees in physical spaces, offering opportunities for hands-on learning, observation, and collaboration. Mentors in this realm engage mentees in face-to-face interactions, providing personalized guidance, feedback, and support that nurtures growth and development. From one-on-one meetings to group sessions, in-person mentors create supportive and nurturing environments that encourage mentees to ask questions, share insights, and seek guidance on their journey. Through their mentorship, they provide mentees with real-world experiences, practical skills, and invaluable life lessons that prepare them for success.

## In-Person Mentorship

In-person mentorship, particularly within the context of spiritual growth, involves face-to-face interactions between the mentor and the mentee. This traditional approach allows for a deeper, more personal connection, fostering trust and understanding in a way that is often more challenging to achieve through remote communication. Regular meetings form the backbone of in-person mentorship, providing structure and continuity for the mentee's spiritual journey. These meetings are typically scheduled weekly, bi-weekly, or monthly, depending on the needs and availability of both parties. Consistent, in-person interactions allow for progressive development, ensuring that the mentee receives ongoing guidance and support. One of the primary benefits of in-person mentorship is the ability to engage in personal interaction. Face-to-face communication enables both mentor and mentee to read body language, facial expressions, and other non-verbal cues.

## THE MENTOR & THE MENTEE

These cues can provide valuable insights into the mentee's emotional and spiritual state, allowing the mentor to address sensitive topics with greater empathy and understanding. The immediate feedback loop created by these interactions is crucial for effective mentorship. In-person mentorship also allows for customized guidance tailored to the specific needs of the mentee. Mentors can develop personalized Bible study plans, and targeted prayer strategies, and offer practical advice on integrating faith into everyday life. This bespoke approach ensures that the mentee receives the most relevant and impactful guidance for their unique spiritual journey. Shared spiritual practices, such as prayer and worship, are another significant aspect of in-person mentorship. Engaging in these activities together deepens the spiritual bond between the mentor and mentee. The shared experience of seeking God's presence and wisdom creates a sense of unity and shared purpose, enhancing the overall mentorship experience. Accountability is more easily maintained through in-person interactions. The mentor can check on the mentee's progress, offer encouragement, and address any struggles or setbacks in a direct and personal manner.

This aspect of mentorship helps ensure that the mentee remain faithful to their spiritual commitments and continue to grow in their faith. Life-on-life discipleship is a unique element of in-person mentorship, where the mentor shares their daily routines and spiritual practices with the mentee. This immersive approach provides the mentee with a living example of what a mature Christian life looks like. By witnessing the mentor's faith in action, the mentee gains practical insights into applying spiritual principles in their own life. The benefits of in-person mentorship are numerous. The personal connection fostered through regular, face-to-face meetings often leads to a more profound and trusting relationship, which is essential for effective mentorship.

## PATIENCE SAKUTUKWA

The ability to offer immediate support and encouragement means that issues can be addressed as they arise, providing real-time feedback and guidance. This immediate support is invaluable in helping the mentee navigate their spiritual journey. In-person mentorship also promotes holistic growth. The mentor can observe and guide the mentee's overall personal development, encompassing spiritual, emotional, and relational growth.

This comprehensive approach ensures that the mentee's development is well-rounded and integrated into all aspects of their life. Furthermore, in-person mentorship facilitates community building. By integrating the mentee into the wider church community, the mentor helps them form connections and find their place within the body of Christ. This sense of belonging is crucial for sustaining long-term spiritual growth and development. Despite its many benefits, in-person mentorship also presents certain challenges. Scheduling conflicts can arise, making it difficult to find mutually convenient times for regular meetings. Additionally, geographical limitations mean that proximity is essential for in-person mentorship, limiting the pool of potential mentors and mentees to those within a reasonable distance. In-person meetings can also be more resource-intensive, requiring time, travel, and sometimes financial investment for meeting places or materials. To overcome these challenges and maximize the effectiveness of in-person mentorship, certain best practices should be followed. Setting clear objectives at the outset helps both mentor and mentee understand the purpose and desired outcomes of their time together.

Maintaining a strong sense of confidentiality is crucial for building trust, allowing the mentee to share openly without fear of judgment or breach of privacy. Developing a structured plan for meetings ensures that time together is productive and focused. This plan might include a mix of Bible study, prayer, discussion of specific topics, and practical application exercises. While structure is important, it is also essential to remain flexible to address the immediate needs and concerns of the mentee. Being willing to adapt the plan in response to what the Holy Spirit is prompting during meetings can lead to more meaningful and impactful interactions.

Ongoing evaluation of the mentorship relationship is vital for ensuring its effectiveness. Regularly assessing progress helps determine if goals are being met and if the mentee is growing spiritually. Making adjustments as needed ensures that the relationship remains beneficial and continues to support the mentee's development. A notable example of the impact of in-person mentorship can be seen in the Navigators' Collegiate Ministry.

This Christian organization has a well-established program that emphasizes in-person mentorship. Mentors, often older students or staff members, invest deeply in the lives of younger students. This approach has proven highly effective in promoting spiritual formation, community engagement, and leadership development. Students involved in this program report significant growth in their personal faith, understanding of scripture, and commitment to Christian principles. The mentorship helps them integrate into the broader faith community on campus, providing a support network that extends beyond the formal mentorship relationship. Many mentees go on to become mentors themselves, perpetuating a cycle of discipleship and leadership within the campus ministry context.

In-person mentorship remains a cornerstone of effective spiritual growth and discipleship. It offers a powerful means to foster deep, transformative relationships grounded in faith. By understanding and leveraging the unique strengths of this approach, mentors can profoundly impact their mentees' spiritual journeys, promoting holistic growth and integration into the broader Christian community.

# Chapter 20

# Academic Mentorship

*"The journey of a thousand miles begins with a single step."* - Lao Tzu
Academic mentorship is focused on educational and intellectual development. It involves a mentor, often a teacher or professor, guiding a student through their academic journey. Academic mentors provide support, advice, and encouragement, helping students achieve their academic goals and develop a passion for learning. The mentor's role in academic mentorship includes offering academic guidance, helping students set and achieve academic goals, and providing feedback on performance. They also offer support with specific academic challenges, such as understanding difficult concepts, preparing for exams, and completing assignments.

Effective academic mentorship involves regular communication, goal setting, and progress tracking. The mentor and mentee work together to identify areas for improvement, develop study strategies, and overcome academic challenges. The mentor provides constructive feedback and support, helping the mentee stay focused and motivated. The benefits of academic mentorship are numerous. Mentees gain valuable insights into their academic field, develop essential study skills, and build confidence in their abilities. They also benefit from the mentor's academic network, gaining access to new opportunities and resources. Academic mentorship can improve academic performance, enhance intellectual development, and foster a lifelong passion for learning.

# Chapter 21

# Cross-Cultural Mentorship

*"A mentor bridges worlds, weaving threads of understanding between cultures to inspire growth, mutual respect, and a legacy of shared wisdom."*

Cross-cultural mentorship involves mentoring relationships between individuals from different cultural backgrounds. This form of mentorship recognizes the value of diverse perspectives and promotes mutual learning and understanding. It fosters cultural exchange, broadens horizons, and enhances intercultural competence. The mentor's role in cross-cultural mentorship includes offering guidance, support, and advice while respecting and appreciating the mentee's cultural background. They help mentees navigate cultural differences, develop intercultural skills, and achieve their goals. Cross-cultural mentorship involves creating an inclusive and respectful environment where cultural diversity is celebrated.

Through cross-cultural exchanges and collaborative projects, individuals from diverse backgrounds come together to learn from one another, to challenge their assumptions, and to broaden their perspectives on the world. As the world becomes increasingly interconnected, the importance of global mentorship cannot be overstated. Through their shared commitment to learning and collaboration, individuals from every corner of effective cross-cultural mentorship requires cultural sensitivity, open communication, and mutual respect. The mentor and mentee must be willing to learn from each other's cultural perspectives, creating a relationship based on mutual understanding and appreciation. Cross-cultural mentorship can be a powerful tool for promoting diversity and inclusion, fostering a culture of respect and collaboration. The benefits of cross-cultural mentorship are numerous. Mentees gain valuable insights and support from their mentors, develop intercultural skills, and build confidence in their abilities. They also benefit from the mentor's network, gaining access to new opportunities and resources.

Cross-cultural mentorship enhances personal and professional development, fosters a sense of belonging, and promotes mutual growth and learning. It also helps build a more inclusive and culturally competent community, promoting understanding and collaboration across cultural boundaries.

# PART V

# UNDERSTANDING MENTORSHIP IMPACT

# Chapter 22

# Mentorship in the Era of Technology

*"The art of communication is the language of leadership."* - James Humes
In today's rapidly evolving world, mentorship has adapted to meet the demands of a technologically advanced society. The digital age has transformed the way we connect, learn, and grow, making mentorship more accessible and dynamic than ever before. This chapter explores what we should expect in modern mentorship and the types of mentorship we should embrace in this era. The advent of technology has expanded the horizons of mentorship, breaking down geographical barriers and enabling connections across the globe. Virtual mentorship, for instance, involves connecting mentors and mentees through online platforms, video calls, and messaging apps. This form of mentorship offers flexibility and convenience, allowing participants to engage from anywhere in the world.

Many organizations and institutions now offer structured online mentorship programs. These programs often include matching algorithms, scheduled virtual meetings, and digital resources to support the mentorship relationship. Additionally, various apps and platforms have been developed to facilitate mentorship. These tools provide features such as goal tracking, feedback mechanisms, and access to a community of mentors and mentees.

Technology has also enabled the creation of global mentorship networks, connecting individuals across different industries, cultures, and time zones. These networks offer diverse perspectives and opportunities for cross-cultural learning, enriching the mentorship experience. To thrive in the era of technology, we must embrace various types of mentorship. Hybrid mentorship, for example, combines in-person and virtual interactions, offering the best of both worlds. It allows for flexible scheduling while maintaining the personal touch of face-to-face meetings. Peer mentorship involves individuals at similar stages in their careers or education supporting each other.

## THE MENTOR & THE MENTEE

This form of mentorship leverages shared experiences and fosters collaborative learning. Reverse mentorship, on the other hand, involves younger or less experienced individuals mentoring more senior colleagues. This approach encourages knowledge sharing in areas such as technology, social media, and contemporary trends. Group mentorship involves one mentor working with multiple mentees simultaneously. This model promotes community building and allows mentees to learn from each other's experiences, creating a dynamic and supportive learning environment. The benefits of technological mentorship are manifold. Technology makes mentorship accessible to a wider audience, including those in remote or underserved areas. It democratizes mentorship opportunities, ensuring more people can benefit from guidance and support. Virtual and online mentorship also offers flexibility in scheduling and communication, accommodating busy lifestyles and diverse time zones. Moreover, global connections facilitated by technology allow mentees to gain insights from diverse cultures and industries, enriching their learning experience.

Digital platforms often provide a wealth of resources, including articles, webinars, and forums, to supplement the mentorship relationship. To effectively leverage technological mentorship, it is crucial to utilize technology effectively. Leverage the available technology to enhance communication, track progress, and access resources. Familiarize yourself with the tools and platforms that best suit your mentorship needs. Schedule regular virtual meetings and stay connected through messaging apps or emails. Consistent communication is key to maintaining a strong mentorship relationship. Clearly define the goals and expectations for the mentorship relationship. Use digital tools to track progress and celebrate milestones. Embrace the flexibility that technology offers and be open to adapting your approach based on the needs and preferences of both mentor and mentee. Despite the virtual nature of the relationship, prioritize building a personal connection. Show empathy, actively listen, and be genuinely invested in each other's growth. In the era of technology, mentorship has evolved to become more accessible, flexible, and diverse.

By embracing modern forms of mentorship, we can create meaningful connections, foster personal and professional growth, and navigate the complexities of the digital age.

# Chapter 23

# Navigating your Mentorship Journey

*"The journey of a thousand miles begins with a single step."* - Lao Tzu

With her mentor by her side, Sarah embarked on a journey of self-discovery and empowerment, guided by the principles of trust, communication, and mutual respect. Together, they navigated the twists and turns of life's labyrinth, overcoming obstacles and seizing opportunities with grace and intention. Through heartfelt conversations and soulful reflections, Sarah and her mentor forged a bond that transcended boundaries, fostering deep personal and professional growth. With each passing day, Sarah felt herself growing stronger, more confident, and more resilient a testament to the transformative power of mentorship.

As she looked out at the city skyline once more, Sarah knew that she had found her guiding light in the luminous embrace of mentorship. For in the boundless expanse of possibility, she had discovered not just a mentor, but a friend, a confidant, and a source of inspiration. And in that moment, she realized that the journey had only just begun.

As we stand at the threshold of our mentorship journey, poised on the brink of transformation, we are faced with a pivotal question: how do we navigate this path with grace and intention? How do we cultivate a relationship that fosters growth, learning, and mutual respect? In this final chapter, we embark on a journey of self-discovery and empowerment, guided by the wisdom of those who have walked this path before us. We explore the principles of effective communication, trust-building, and goal-setting, laying the groundwork for a transformative mentorship journey. Through heartfelt anecdotes and soulful reflections, we uncover the secrets to nurturing a mentorship relationship that transcends boundaries and fosters deep personal and professional growth.

Together, let us embrace the transformative power of mentorship, as we embark on a journey of self-discovery, growth, and empowerment. For in the luminous embrace of mentorship's guiding light, we find not just direction, but a sense of purpose, belonging, and fulfillment. Navigating the mentorship journey is an exciting and rewarding experience that requires patience, perseverance, and a willingness to embrace the unknown. Whether you're embarking on a new mentorship relationship or deepening an existing one, there are certain principles to keep in mind as you navigate the ups and downs of the journey ahead. First and foremost, it's important to approach mentorship with an open mind and a humble heart. Be willing to listen, learn, and grow from the insights and experiences of your mentor or mentee, and be open to feedback and constructive criticism along the way. Remember that mentorship is a collaborative effort, and it's important to cultivate a relationship based on trust, respect, and mutual understanding. It's also important to set clear goals and expectations for the mentorship relationship, outlining what you hope to achieve and how you plan to work together to accomplish your shared objectives.

Whether you're seeking guidance on a specific project, skill development, or personal growth, having a clear roadmap will help keep you focused and motivated as you navigate the challenges and opportunities of the mentorship journey. Finally, don't be afraid to seek support and guidance from others as you navigate your mentorship journey. Whether it's connecting with other mentors and mentees for advice and inspiration or seeking out resources and tools to support your growth and development, remember that you're not alone on this journey. By embracing the power of mentorship and surrounding yourself with a supportive community of like-minded individuals, you'll be well-equipped to navigate the challenges and opportunities that lie ahead on your path to personal and professional fulfillment.

In the tapestry of human experience, mentorship emerges as a guiding thread, weaving its way through the fabric of our lives, connecting us to a lineage of wisdom, inspiration, and growth. Throughout this book, we have explored the myriad forms and facets of mentorship, from the spiritual realms of inner exploration to the practical domains of career advancement.

We have witnessed the transformative power of mentorship in the lives of individuals across diverse backgrounds and contexts, from budding artists finding their creative voice to seasoned professionals navigating the complexities of the modern workplace. At its heart, mentorship is more than just a relationship; it is a sacred covenant between mentor and mentee, a bond forged in the crucible of trust, respect, and shared aspiration. It is a journey of mutual learning and growth, where both mentor and mentee embark on a quest for knowledge, insight, and self-discovery. As we bring our exploration of mentorship to a close, let us carry forward the lessons learned and the insights gained into our own lives and communities.

Let us seek out opportunities to mentor and be mentored, to share our wisdom and experience with those who come after us, and to learn from the wisdom of those who have walked the path before us. For in the end, mentorship is not just about passing down knowledge or achieving personal success; it is about building a brighter, more compassionate world for future generations one guided by the timeless principles of wisdom, generosity, and mutual respect.

# THE MENTOR & THE MENTEE

# PART VI

# GLOBAL CASE STUDIES

# Chapter 24

# CASE STUDY 1

### Youth Mentorship Initiative in India

In the heart of rural Maharashtra, where lush landscapes often belie the harsh realities of limited access to education and opportunities, the Youth Mentorship Initiative (YMI) has emerged as a beacon of hope. In these villages, poverty and systemic challenges frequently shroud the aspirations of young minds. Yet, amidst these adversities, YMI is rewriting the story of countless lives by empowering the next generation through mentorship. The initiative began with a vision shared by a group of former educators who understood the transformative power of guidance and support. Determined to bridge the gap between urban resources and rural needs, they created YMI as a platform to connect young professionals from cities with high school students in underserved villages.

These mentors brought with them not only their expertise but also a sense of hope and belief that every dream, no matter how distant it seemed, could become a reality. One of the most inspiring stories from YMI is that of Priya, a farmer's daughter whose dreams of becoming an engineer seemed like an unattainable fantasy. Priya excelled in mathematics and science, but with limited access to resources, her aspirations were confined to the pages of her schoolbooks. Enter Rohan, a software engineer from Mumbai, who became her mentor through YMI.

Rohan's role extended far beyond academic support. He introduced Priya to online learning platforms that opened her eyes to a world of possibilities, from coding tutorials to scholarship opportunities. Rohan's guidance didn't stop there; he also taught Priya how to draft compelling scholarship applications and prepared her for interviews. With his mentorship, Priya secured a prestigious scholarship, paving the way for her to pursue computer science at one of India's top universities. Today, Priya stands on the brink of a promising career in technology, a testament to the transformative power of mentorship.

The YMI program is rooted in the belief that mentorship is more than just sharing knowledge. It is about fostering confidence, resilience, and a belief in one's potential. Mentors, who are often professionals in fields ranging from engineering to healthcare, travel from urban areas to rural schools to conduct workshops, one-on-one sessions, and motivational talks. These interactions have become a lifeline for students who often lack role models in their immediate environment.

For the mentors, the experience is equally profound. Many describe their involvement as a journey of personal growth, where they gain a deeper understanding of rural India's challenges while contributing meaningfully to the nation's development. The bond between mentor and mentee often transcends the formal framework of the program, evolving into lifelong connections rooted in mutual respect and shared goals. The impact of YMI extends beyond individual success stories. Entire communities are transformed as students like Priya break free from the cycle of poverty and become role models for their peers.

Parents who once hesitated to invest in their children's education now see it as a pathway to a better future. Teachers, inspired by the program's success, collaborate with mentors to create more enriching learning environments. The Youth Mentorship Initiative's model has proven to be both scalable and sustainable, thanks to its innovative use of technology and partnerships. Digital tools allow mentors to remain connected with their mentees long after their in-person visits, ensuring continuous support. Collaborations with local schools and NGOs help identify students in need and provide logistical support for the program's implementation.

YMI's success is a poignant reminder of the power of mentorship to change lives. In rural Maharashtra, where dreams once faded in the face of adversity, they now shine brightly, lighting the way for others to follow. Through its unwavering commitment to nurturing young talent, YMI has not only transformed individual lives but has also sown the seeds for a brighter and more equitable future for India.

# CASE STUDY 2
### Indigenous Youth Mentorship Program in Canada

The *Indigenous Youth Mentorship Program (IYMP)* in Manitoba, Canada, seeks to empower Indigenous youth by preserving their cultural heritage while fostering leadership skills. Led by elders and community leaders, IYMP combines traditional knowledge with modern education.

Maria, a Cree teenager, discovered her passion for environmental science through the program's workshops on sustainable land practices. Her mentor, a university professor with Cree heritage, encouraged her to apply for a scholarship, which she successfully secured. Programs like IYMP exemplify the integration of mentorship with cultural preservation, aligning with recommendations by the Truth and Reconciliation Commission of Canada (2015).

# CASE STUDY 3

### Social Entrepreneurship Mentorship in Brazil

In São Paulo, Brazil, the *Social Entrepreneurship Mentorship (SEM)* program is inspiring change by training youth to address societal challenges through innovation. Run by local NGOs, SEM emphasizes sustainable development and poverty alleviation.

Carlos, a young mentee, developed a mobile app to connect homeless individuals with available shelters and services. His mentor, a tech entrepreneur, provided him with technical expertise and helped pitch the project to investors. Carlos' app has been adopted citywide, showcasing the profound impact of social entrepreneurship on urban challenges. The Brazilian Entrepreneurship Review (2023) highlights SEM as a model for other nations.

Sophia, a mentee passionate about marine life, worked with her mentor, a marine biologist, to design community workshops on protecting coral reefs. Her efforts gained national recognition, inspiring many young Australians to engage in conservation work. The Australian Journal of Environmental Studies (2022) underscores the importance of mentorship in fostering a new generation of environmental advocates.

# CASE STUDY 4

**Nelson Mandela Fellowship**

The *Nelson Mandela Fellowship* is a prestigious mentorship program aimed at fostering leadership across Africa. Established in honor of Nelson Mandela's legacy, the program selects young leaders annually, providing them with training, mentorship, and networking opportunities to champion social justice and economic development. Lerato, a fellow from South Africa, initiated a community project to combat gender-based violence. Her mentor, a prominent human rights lawyer, guided her in creating legal frameworks to support survivors. The Nelson Mandela Foundation (2023) notes that the fellowship exemplifies Mandela's belief in the transformative power of mentorship to build resilient societies.

# PART VII

# CONCLUSION & ADDITIONAL RESOURCES

# CONCLUSION

*"In the symphony of life, mentorship is the melody that resonates across generations, harmonizing wisdom, growth, and purpose."*

As we draw the curtain on this exploration of mentorship, we reflect on the profound journey we've taken together—a journey through the heart of what it means to guide, be guided, and evolve. The lessons we've unearthed are timeless: mentorship transcends cultural boundaries, bridges generational divides, and ignites the spark of potential in each of us. Mentorship is not merely a relationship; it is a transformational journey a sacred bond where both mentor and mentee emerge enriched, empowered, and enlightened. It is a beacon of hope in a world often overwhelmed by complexities, a guiding light that helps us navigate the labyrinth of our lives.

This book is a testament to the enduring power of mentorship. It is a call to action, urging us to embrace this incredible gift, share our experiences, and cultivate spaces where mentorship can flourish. Whether you are stepping into the shoes of a mentor or seeking the wisdom of one, remember that the path of mentorship is one of mutual growth and shared triumphs. May this book inspire you to embark on your mentorship journey with courage, curiosity, and compassion. As you step into the future, let mentorship guide you toward a life of purpose and fulfillment. Together, as mentors and mentees, we hold the power to shape a brighter, more connected, and compassionate world. Throughout these pages, we have explored the myriad facets of mentorship, from its origins in ancient wisdom to its modern-day manifestations in diverse spheres of life. We have delved into the qualities of effective mentors and mentees, the different types of mentorship relationships, and the myriad benefits that mentorship brings to individuals, communities, and society as a whole.

At its core, mentorship is a sacred dance of growth and learning, where mentors and mentees come together to share insights, experiences, and aspirations, and to walk hand in hand along the path of personal and professional development. It is a relationship built on trust, respect, and mutual understanding, where mentors serve as guides, confidants, and champions for their mentees, empowering them to overcome obstacles, seize opportunities, and achieve their full potential. As we reflect on the journey of mentorship, it becomes clear that its impact extends far beyond the individual participants, shaping the course of history and leaving an indelible mark on the fabric of society. As we bid farewell to these pages, let us carry forth the lessons and insights we have gleaned on our mentorship journey.

Let us cultivate a spirit of curiosity, humility, and compassion as we seek out mentors and mentees to walk beside us on the path of life. And let us remember that in the sacred dance of mentorship, we are not just shaping our own destinies, but also the destiny of future generations, leaving behind a legacy of wisdom, kindness, and hope for all who come after us.

# BIBLIOGRAPHY

- Erikson, Millard J. *Christian Theology*. Grand Rapids: Baker Academic, 1998.
- Covey, Stephen R. *The 7 Habits of Highly Effective People*. New York: Free Press, 1989.
- Humes, James. *The Art of Communication: The Language of Leadership*. New York: HarperCollins, 2012.
- Lao Tzu. *Tao Te Ching*. Translation by Stephen Mitchell. New York: Harper Perennial, 1988.

**Research and Reports**

- "The Effects of Mentorship on Career Success." *Journal of Applied Psychology*, Vol. 85, No. 3, 2021.
- "Technological Advances in Mentorship: Trends and Opportunities." *Harvard Business Review*, March 2023.

**Scriptures and Spiritual Reflections**

- The Bible (New International Version). Relevant scriptures cited throughout the book, including Proverbs 27:17 ("As iron sharpens iron, so one person sharpens another.")

**Online and Digital Resources**

- LinkedIn Learning. "Mentorship in the Digital Age: Tools and Techniques." Accessed June 2024.
- Mentorship.com. "Global Networks and Their Role in Shaping Mentorship." Accessed July 2024.

# THE MENTOR & THE MENTEE

## Personal Reflections and Anecdotes

- Stories and reflections shared by mentors and mentees featured throughout the chapters, including Sarah's transformative mentorship journey.

## Inspirational **Quotes**

- Emerson, Ralph Waldo. "Our chief want is someone who will inspire us to be what we know we could be."
- Maya Angelou. "When we learn, teach. When we get, give."

## Case Study References

1. **NITI Aayog**: *Atal Innovation Mission*. Retrieved from www.niti.gov.in[1]
2. **Teach for India**: Impact reports and testimonials from www.teachforindia.org[2]
3. **The Lighthouse Project**: Case studies available on www.lighthouseproject.in[3]
4. **National Skill Development Corporation (NSDC)**: Reports on vocational training impact retrieved from www.nsdcindia.org[4]
5. Secondary literature on youth mentorship effectiveness from journals on education and skill development in India.

---

1. https://www.niti.gov.in
2. https://www.teachforindia.org
3. https://www.lighthouseproject.in
4. https://www.nsdcindia.org

PATIENCE SAKUTUKWA

# THE END

# Don't miss out!

Visit the website below and you can sign up to receive emails whenever Patience Sakutukwa publishes a new book. There's no charge and no obligation.

https://books2read.com/r/B-A-UYOEB-VUDED

**BOOKS 2 READ**

Connecting independent readers to independent writers.

## About the Author

Patience Sakutukwa, visionary author of "Matters of the Heart" Editions 1-3 and CEO of Lepa Group of Companies, Bethel Publishing House, and Lepaprop Real Estate. As the founder of the God of Bethel International Ministries, she leads with purpose. Patience is also a theological studies student at Tyndale University, an international intercessor, marriage counselor, and passionate youth advocate. She mentors the Zimbabwean Baseball Club Youth, recognizing the youth as the current church, not just the future. In addition to her corporate success, Patience is a Christian filmmaker and the insightful host of the Sisterhood Talkshow. The show, set to air soon on TBNAfrica & TBN Canada, focuses on women in ministry and those who love Jesus, expanding its reach and influence.

www.ingramcontent.com/pod-product-compliance
Lightning Source LLC
Chambersburg PA
CBHW071507040426
42444CB00008B/1527